THESE RADICAL
CHILDREN OF ABRAHAM

THESE RADICAL CHILDREN OF ABRAHAM

LARRY LOVELAW

TATE PUBLISHING & *Enterprises*

Published by Tate Publishing & Enterprises, LLC
127 E. Trade Center Terrace | Mustang, Oklahoma 73064 USA
1.888.361.9473 | www.tatepublishing.com

Tate Publishing is committed to excellence in the publishing industry. The company reflects the philosophy established by the founders, based on Psalms 68:11,
"The Lord gave the word and great was the company of those who published it."

Book design copyright © 2007 by Tate Publishing, LLC. All rights reserved.

Published in the United States of America

ISBN: 978-1-60247-575-5
1. Biblical Studies: Commentary
08.04.16

FOREWORD

Can an everyday Believer overcome the flesh and the opposing spirits of this life?

Larry Lovelaw, the author of "These Radical Children of Abraham" who has been involved in hands-on spiritual warfare for well over 25 years says, "Yes"–and, "Yes, indeed!"

Born and raised in Edinburgh, Scotland, Larry completed an average secondary education, sundry Commercial Practise Studies, including Underwriting and Basic Scots Law. Initially (as a hobby) Larry trained as an instructor in hand to hand combat, which practise became his first love. After immigrating to North America in 1970AD, Larry became a full-time instructor. In the late seventies, Larry experienced that gift, known only to those who kneel before God in the name that is above all names and ask, in all humility, for the spirit of Truth to live within.

He also asked the Most High for wisdom, love, joy, peace, long-suffering, gentleness, meekness, goodness, temperance and faith. Were they granted? Was wisdom granted? Guided by Him who is the way, the truth and the life, Larry began a spiritual journey that can only be described as a tremendous adventure. He left his first love when he heard a voice whisper in his right ear during a meeting, saying words something like this,

"Tell your wife you're going to give up teaching hand-to hand combat."

Larry, believing that he had heard from the Lord, obeyed. Larry was always obsessed with 'getting to the bottom of things' and finding out the truth. Larry mixed experience with much research, outreach and prayer. While wrestling with principalities in a North American city, he found himself, his associates and his loved ones subjected to ongoing counterattacks by unseen forces. When his son's life was suddenly taken in an unfortunate 'accident', he realised that the principalities he'd been fighting were not simply spirits that couldn't fight back and so he set his mind and heart to learning how to first protect himself and his loved ones and then how to carry the fight back to the dark powers that he calls 'the hinderers', quoting the passage, "You did run well; who hindered you?"

In a quiet moment of reflection during intercessory prayer, Larry suddenly realised that his son's unfortunate death was no accident, but was nothing other than a direct and deliberate counterattack caused by unseen forces. He actually stood up in great anger, shaking his fist at the unseen principality and shouting,

"You killed my son! Come down and fight!"

The fact is that, for quite a few years last century, Larry had been simply praying against the evil that he had perceived was afflicting the people of that Northern city and he hadn't properly associated the difficulties that seemed to plague him with counterattacks resulting from his own intercession.

Larry had been using picture language prayers from the Scriptures to come against the evil he saw afflicting his countrymen, friends and neighbours. Then he had a dream where a large raging warrior came rushing towards him all melting and burning like wax, which was synonymous with certain Scriptures he'd used during prayer. Over a period of mishaps and difficulties, during which he felt God was guiding him (through dreams, circumstances, study of Scriptures, etc.) Larry began to realise that he was being trained on how to war in the spirit but was meantime also warned by two separate dreams to 'hold fire' for the moment. A long period of difficulties, with many temptations and ongoing problems convinced Larry that he was a marked man. He felt like one of the followers of Moses that were kept extra busy making bricks so that the Pharaoh would not have to let them go. It seemed that nothing he did succeeded because awkward 'circumstances' kept hindering. He found that his everyday necessities were often provided miraculously instead of by his own efforts. Following the will of God became everything to him but he knew that he fell far, far short of the necessary standard. He found himself helping many different groups and ministries. Helping others to succeed, rather than moving in any personal agenda, seemed to be the direction that God was moving him.

In God's timing, he found the material, that was to become a book, coming together and he diligently kept notes on the ongoing spiritual battles he had to fight in order to set others free and, as it were, to simply keep his own head above water.

On the night when his son drowned, Larry had been chauffeuring his ex-instructor from the airport to a combat-training course venue and had booked a motel for that night. Larry had just informed the old instructor of God's directive to quit hand to hand combat. Larry then decided to just sleep in his own collapsible car-seat.

It was warm summer evening and he thought, 'Why pay for a room when I'm just as comfortable in my own car?'

About 10.30pm, having driven all day, Larry laid back feeling very tired. As he closed his drowsy eyes he distinctly heard that voice whispering, "You should pray for your son." Larry made a mental note to pray more for his teenage son and then drifted off to sleep. It didn't seem like an urgent exhortation at the time.

The next day, he and his old instructor drove the six hour journey to Larry's home town, where he found his wife absent. There were also several notes, posted on their outside door. The people informed him that his son had gone out with a friend in a rowing boat at about 10.30pm the night before and that the boat had capsized and that his son had not yet been found. Larry's wife had already taken the daily one hour flight down to the area where their son had disappeared into the dark waters. Larry, of course, was devastated but went off to find his other (eight year old) son, who had been left with his wife's friends.

The 'friends' went out to a religious meeting, telling

Larry that he should play Monopoly in order to keep his mind off of the tragedy.

Larry complied with their instructions for a few minutes before he came to his senses and, with his other son, he began to grieve the loss of the seventeen year-old.

He was crying out in pain, something like this, "Aaaangg, My son - my son!" when suddenly, he sensed a voice coming up, as it were, from his own belly saying, "He's with me."–and the grief was miraculously, and immediately, gone! Then, a few minutes later, as Larry's thoughts began to drift back to the reality of his older son's death, the grief manifested again. Once again he cried out in anguish, "Aaaangg, My son - my son!" and, suddenly, again he sensed, as it were, that same voice coming up from his own belly saying, "He's with me."–the grief, quite miraculously, vanquished again! This happened quite a few times during the evening until his wife's friends returned.

These friends insisted that Larry should eat something but he refused their offer. They persisted in insisting that he had to have something in his stomach and, because of the persistence of their insistence, he finally agreed to drink a quarter of a cup of milk. They told him that he should leave his younger son with them and just go home and try to get some sleep.

Larry complied meekly and drove off but had to pull over to the side of the road to vomit up the milk that had been pushed on him by these well-meaning people. He was home in bed before midnight and, surprisingly, fell asleep right away.

At about 3.15am, Larry felt the Lord awaken him and give him instructions to pray for certain dignitaries in England, totally unrelated to his own situation, which request puzzled him. Nonetheless he complied, got up, went through to the living room and knelt near the couch to pray.

That area was the same 'prayer spot' from where he had been accustomed to interceding for the city, over the last few months, binding the evil influences that he had discerned were over that area. It was only when he had finished the appointed prayer task that he stood up and considered what must have happened.

The facts of the matter slowly dawned on him and that was when he spoke out in great anger, shaking his fist at the principality and shouting, "You killed my son! Come down and fight!" Of course there was no perceivable reaction but only the silence of the night.

Larry stood there in the semi-darkness feeling anguished, devastated, frustrated, angry and weary all at the same time. His weariness started to overtake him and he realised he was about to go to bed, to sleep—right after having challenged an evil and very real principality to come and fight!

The new revelation of the reality of such a spiritual being that was obviously able to cause great harm to a man caused him to hesitate and decide that, before returning to his bed, he'd better ask for protection from the Lord.

Accordingly, quoting the Scriptures, he asked that the angel of the Lord would encamp round about him; that no weapon formed against him would prosper; that, if the enemy would come against him one way, then the enemy would flee seven ways, with his feet upon slippery ground and with the angel of the Lord chasing him about. After several other prayerful scriptural exhortations and requests, Larry slowly turned and shuffled his way into the dark twilight of their bedroom.

That was when it happened. That was when he saw it! As he sat down on his bed, Larry saw something that made him gasp in dumbfounded amazement.

The corner of the bedroom was about twelve feet from where he had just sat down and there, staring at him from that corner was the image of a face! For some reason, known only to God, Larry was more puzzled than afraid. He was just staring open-mouthed at the spectre with a 'What on earth is that?' expression on his face.

His mind was barely coping with the paranormal experience that his mental perception was trying to come to grips with. He knew that he wasn't dreaming because he had been awake for about half an hour, praying for a well-known political figure. This manifestation just didn't 'compute' with anything within Larry's experience! The face was about twice the size of a normal man but it looked black and metallic with something like glowing, red coals for eyes. Some years later, when the Star Wars movie was advertised, Larry's eyebrows went up and he pointed at a poster of 'Darth Vader' and said, "That is exactly like what I saw that night when the demonic spirit attacked me!"

Actually, it wasn't exactly the same but it was very similar to the movie face of DV depicted in the 'Star Wars' movie released several years later. On the night that the apparition appeared, Larry's room was very dark so that, though he could have seen a book if he'd held it up, he wouldn't have been able to read any writing. Of course he wasn't holding a book or anything. He was just gaping, nonplussed at something that he simply didn't understand!

The apparition, at the moment that Larry had noticed it, had started to glide, very, very slowly and very directly, towards him. It was a really menacing–looking entity, dark and emanating evil from its very presence, but Larry recalled later that he wasn't so much afraid as he was frozen with amazement like a rabbit watching a snake slithering towards it! This just didn't compute! It had traveled towards him about one third of the distance from its starting place in the corner of the room when Larry heard that voice again!

It had seemed like a long time but actually, it was only about seven or eight seconds after the apparition initially appeared when that voice, rising up from Larry's belly, spoke and said, through Larry, something like this; "As David slew Goliath, so shall my words destroy you, O spirit of darkness. As the stone from David's sling struck Goliath in the forehead and brought him down, so do my words strike you and bring you down this very night!"

Larry says that he didn't think to take note and memorize exactly what he had spoken at that moment but, in any case, immediately the words had been spoken, he saw the red glow (in the apparition's eyes) dim down and go out. Then the whole of its face slipped slightly sideways to its left, as if it had sunk about one third down into something like (spiritual quicksand?).

Larry squinted in puzzlement. What on earth was going on?

Still staring nonplussed, Larry saw that the face was almost immediately replaced by another, even stranger, face. The new head was about the size and shape of a horse's head. It had large dark grasshopper-like eyes and somehow Larry could sense that it had large fangs, though its mouth wasn't open.

It was still moving menacingly towards him and Larry was still in his original state of great astonishment. Larry said afterwards that he didn't understand why, though he did have a (subconscious?) sense of great danger, he had no feelings of fear, but only amazement. As the spectre approached more closely–about halfway towards Larry from the corner–he again heard that voice from his belly beginning to say, with real words, something very similar to what was said previously, beginning with, "As David slew Goliath…- But at that moment it seemed that something (like the image of a large TV screen) jumped out from the second apparition and took up a position near the bottom of Larry's bed. Larry, being startled, turned his head towards this new phenomenon.

It was something like a screen featuring the torso of a fancily-dressed go-go dancer, or perhaps a belly dancer, jiggling around in a red and gold dancing costume. However, the torso of the dancer had no limbs or head attached!

attention had been momentarily distracted from nd apparition and his (intended?) words had been naited in mid-sentence when, suddenly, there was nothing anywhere in the room. He looked around. Nothing. The silence of the darkness roared like a vast empty cavern.

Larry's comment, after several moments taken to gather his sensibilities was, "Wow!," and, then, after a few more moments he remembers asking himself,

"What on earth was that?"

It was an experience that he could not deny. He had been wide awake and on his way to go to bed so it wasn't a dream and he knew that this was not simply imagination. What on earth happened that night? Later, looking at things logically, Larry says that he reckons some kind of spiritual being had responded to his angry challenge and had come to destroy him 'somehow'. However, in answer to his request for the Lord to protect him and possibly by the actual declaration of inspired warfare scriptures, the Lord had not allowed him to be destroyed.

Larry speculates that, because he gave the enemy permission, by the words of his original challenge, that spectre had felt legally justified in attacking him.

Larry makes this conjecture: "It was probably some kind of two-headed demonic spirit-being. The first 'head' manifested as the DV-like apparition and was simply defeated by a declaration that brought it down. The second 'head' then manifested in another horrible form but, when faced with the same problem of being linked to a Scriptural warfare barrage in which it must lose, chose to use a distraction technique. That effectively caused my attention to be turned away." Somehow, Larry reckons that the breaking of continuity of speech and concentration, gave the second 'head' an opportunity to make good its escape. Whether the visual images presented reflected the real form of the demon/s or was simply two scary images put forward by them as a front, is a moot point. They, (or it) were (or was) defeated by simply linking the situation to victory experienced in the Word of God.

Later, when sharing the experience with others after a men's prayer meeting, Larry was surprised at some of the reactions. Some were not even surprised, not showing any real interest as if that sort of thing happened every day! Some were very quick to change the subject to something they felt more comfortable with, and one man, with obvious sarcasm and envy, sneeringly indicated that now Larry was a special spiritual hero, 'greater than all the others at the meeting'. Such a concept had never even occurred to Larry because, if anything, he'd felt almost like a childish spectator during the whole confrontation and certainly no hero! It didn't occur to Larry at the time that spirits can attack using such things as discouragement and scorn through friends, family and even church, synagogue or mosque members!

Of course there were a few men at the meeting who saw the discourse on the event as something positive where a dark enemy of the people of God had been defeated by the grace and action of the Lord. These men then, of course, placed the experience on their spiritual memory shelves, just in case something similar happened to them. That seemed to be the wise way to treat such a phenomenon.

Larry, for a very short while thereafter, continued his prayer attacks on the principalities but claims he was consequently warned in two separate dreams to cease because he simply wasn't ready and perhaps wouldn't fare so well in future encounters if he didn't wait for the time being, at least.

He finally got the message and made his ongoing intercession more geared towards protection of the saints than towards ongoing aggression against the evil that was all around. Larry had a theory that, because of that confrontation, there were certain spiritual hinderers assigned directly to him that were allowed to create problems for him specifically for many years.

There is a Scripture that many have treated as if it were a rhetorical question but that is more likely a little hint to teach the people of God what part of their problem is. When one fails in their walk with the Lord, is it ever caused by 'hinderers?'

"Ye did run well; who did hinder you… ?" Galatians 5:7

The truth is that God has made a way!

Many commentaries look at the question posed in Galatians 5:7 as a rhetorical exhortation to do better or to recognise that some physical person had seduced the reader by wrong doctrine or the like, which is no doubt one application of that Scripture. However, it seems to be a rare commentary that places the blame on the same lap as did Eve, who had failed in her spiritual walk with God. When Eve placed the blame squarely on the back of the serpent (though I'm not sure whether serpents have shoulders to lay the blame onto or not) then God pronounced judgement on the one who'd hindered her spiritual walk. That seemed to Larry to be a good place to start, looking forward to the time when these hinderers would all be judged.

Larry became convinced that there were specific, real, nameable, spiritual beings that were hindering, meddling and attacking everything he did, from his own commercial undertakings to his personal relationships. These hinderers even tried to curtail his walk with the Spirit of the Word, who states, "Be ye holy, for I am holy." He also knew that he wasn't the only one being 'hindered' in this way.

Was there a way to overcome these hinderers?

In addition to studying relevant passages throughout Scripture, Larry did much meditating on the memory of that apparition which was apparently 'defeated by a declaration that brought it down'. The principle seemed to be that the Word of God is quick and powerful and sharper than any two-edged sword.

Larry wondered:

"Can spiritual beings be defeated simply by speaking words,

just as, by the sword, a physical enemy can be defeated?"

Though author Larry Lovelaw says that he often laid awake in the late evenings, and in the early mornings, listening to the silence, remaining open to Rhema words from the Lord, while also meditating on words pertaining to spiritual warfare that would bring truth into print, he did not set out initially to write a book. Instead, his ongoing notes seemed to come together in a lucid way, which led to an organised format that he had made available temporarily on a web site for a number of years.

When he found himself to be semi-retired from commerce, Larry felt led to look for another way to make the information more generally available. He also felt that he was led by the Lord to accept the offer to publish. The rest is ongoing history.

Hopefully, dear reader you, like the publisher, will see the great value that some of the concepts in this book can offer to those who are able to receive, especially for the purposes of spiritual warfare at the end of this age, which is certainly nearer than when you first started reading this foreword.

Larry and his beloved wife often read the Scriptures together after praying for guidance and asking for elucidation. Using a principle found in the Book of Daniel, they also share and compare their dreams with each other. That principle, of course can be applied to wherever you walk and to whatever you are led to read.

I know that Larry would exhort you to pray to the Lord for understanding, especially whenever reading any book containing words from the Word of God.

It has been said that his book, "These Radical Children

of Abraham" can be read over and over with great benefit because it contains so much of the Word.

I personally hope and trust that you, with Larry Lovelaw, will continue to ask God directly to give you ongoing elucidation, wisdom and understanding, in addition to love, joy, peace, long-suffering, gentleness, goodness, faith, meekness and temperance; against which there is no law. SHALOM

PREFACE

These Radical Children of Abraham

This book is unusual both in its composition and in its emphases. 'Worship truth', says the sage, 'and you will please God'. 'What is truth?' answers the politician. It is the glory of God to conceal a thing but it is the honour of kings to search out a matter. Now, what on earth does that mean? Has Larry Lovelaw put his finger on some hidden truth? Read on.

Truth can be stranger than fiction but the overcomer chooses to dismantle traditional shelves of understanding in order to install hardware that supports truth. Who is willing to turn from nurtured fantasies to liberty in reality? Religion that has crept into churches has not always truly benefited the widows and the orphans. Churchmen like their pews, mosquitoes like their swamps, but the faithful seek after reality in truth. Pride obstructs truth but love is humble and true. Pride says, "Don't listen to what I don't want you to believe" but Love says, "How can I understand and how can I then help my brother to understand truth?" Truth and love are covenant partners but pride wants neither. If pride is your master, unless you want to break free, there is no point in reading on. Then again, perhaps the proud may be educated by this book to desire personal liberty and to desire truth, with love by God. Perhaps elucidation will set the prideful free.

Pride will never allow this statement: "If I have been wrong, I will change so that I may be right. I am open to the truth of God and to receive correction where I have been in error." Pride is the leviathan who opposes love and truth and that is an interesting study in itself. The love of truth emanates from the deep reverence of the Lord, which is the beginning of wisdom. Does pride allow wisdom or does pride grip tradition like a monkey's fist trapped in a bottleneck? Decide!

Many things are explained clearly, beginning necessarily with the detailing of each system of belief that is built upon the covenant of Abraham, the father of the faithful. Logically, Lovelaw leads us to the basic tenets of truth in God. In comparing these three faiths, the author examines them first logically, then critically, bringing out the motivations, ideals, concepts and goals of each, which necessarily manifest in the actions of their followers. Lovelaw even finds areas of agreement, insisting that their mutual enemy is not human but is spiritual. He makes somewhat revelationary (for some) observations such as that, while all three of these faiths are mutually based upon the covenant of Abraham, their basic tenets differ. All three commonly are against libertinism. All three faiths claim the promises of God given to Abraham of liberating his offspring from the bondage of sin, which bondage is a tyranny over the mind of man. "To build upon the words of Thomas Jefferson, in fulfilling these goals we are pledged to wage unending holy struggle (jihâd) against every form of tyranny over the mind of man." (Mission Statement of the Minaret of

Freedom Institute). Yet Lovelaw claims, by his conclusions, that all three faiths cannot, ever, be melded together to agree, for at least one of them is exclusive to the others, being directly in opposition to their doctrines.

All three faiths express a desire to submit to God and 'for love of God' they follow what they believe will please Him. In his book, 'These Radical Children of Abraham', Lovelaw claims that they cannot all three be right and he examines their individual prayers and their interpretation of what really happened so many centuries back when God acted on His decision to move through his covenant seed to bless the Children of Abraham. "Let's all get in step with the truth of God!"

The faithful have been oppressed since they began to believe but, like the people of Esther, favoured by the king, in the days of Ahasuerus the king of Persia, there is a time to rise up and fight back in the spirit with words that cut through the ropes of bondage as with a sword. Like Haman, Satan is the common enemy. Is it time to put a hood over the head of Haman that he may no longer harass the King's lady? Is it time for the lady to request that the dead sons of Haman be strung up on their own gallows? 'Them thar's fightin' words ol' buddy!' - 'Yup!' Well, are we to fight the good fight or lapse into greater bondage, wasting our time gathering straw to make bricks for our enemies? With analogies and parables the Lord has spoken, giving powerful weapons to His people, for His words are the spirit sword and His words are our weapons in the realm of the spirit. But when He returns, will He find faith on the earth? (So asked the Prince of princes, who is the predicted Messiah in the prophetic words of Daniel)[.]

With much insight and understanding, the author also speaks plainly and asks many relevant questions with obvious answers that open up new battlefronts in a field where victory is assured.

This book These Radical Children of Abraham…

- Offers a challenge to face truth rather than tradition; yet adheres to many traditional values.
- Creates a renewed respect for God and opens doors to things hidden from the beginning.
- Challenges the apathetic among us and educates the ignorant, if such would even read it.
- Offers people who are presently Muslims, Christians or Jews a way to triumph over evil.
- Exposes the effectual threat of fundamentalist lumping.
- Is what you need to know to win the spiritual battle for our souls, begun centuries ago.
- Speaks of a battle which must not be lost.
- Builds shelves of understanding, line upon line, precept upon precept, here a little, there a little.
- Offers new and refreshing insight into spiritual warfare.
- Puts a sword, as it were, in the hands of the good wrestlers before the fight ensues and, if they know and understand their weapons and their enemy then their victory is assured!
- Makes clear the way to battle in the spirit and,

almost as an afterthought, gives clear direction how to better pray for real protection for yourself and your loved ones.

- Pinpoints the enemy of every believer, with exhortation and explanation on how to shake off the bands of our common enemy—the enemy of all mankind, and to provide liberty without libertinism to the faithful.

The readers' advantage is as the advantage of those who wield words inspired by God, as directed by God, who cannot lose for the end has already been written in the Book! There have been inner struggles but now is the time for victory for God's people! Are we not all children of the living God, who loves us all? As a sword in the hand of the faithful, so is a message of words spoken in faith.

"Face truth, accept truth become one with truth, move with truth—and truth will set us free!"

Are y'all ready for that?

Read on…

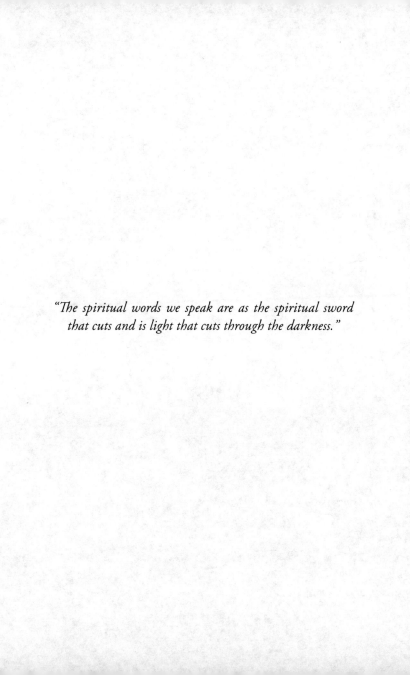

"The spiritual words we speak are as the spiritual sword that cuts and is light that cuts through the darkness."

"WE MUSLIMS, CHRISTIANS AND JEWS CAN ALL AGREE ON AT LEAST ONE THING!"

All three of these religious groups would admit that the Creator of all things spoke to Abraham, the husband of Sarah, and commanded him to sacrifice his son as a test of faith and obedience.

However, the majority of people, including many 'Jews and Christians', have simply believed a lie!

Many Westerners have believed that 'Allah' is just the Arabic name for their God.

Christians have been heard to say, "Jesus is the only way to Allah". This statement is, at worst, a deliberately misleading and dangerous lie or, at very least, a heavy misconception! (See page 44)

ISLAM

Islam is a religion that was started in the seventh century AD, reputedly by a man named Mohammed, though some adherents do boast that they can prove that the 'roots of Islam' reach all the way back to the fabled and mystical Babylonian era!

'AD' means Anno Domini, which is Latin for 'In the year of our Lord'. Our modern calendar is dated from the time of Jesus Christ (AD) and the era before that is referred to as BC (before Christ).

Modern day Islam was conceived and evolved therefore, 'in the year of our Lord' (referring to Jesus Christ), around 600 AD or, a little over 600 years after Christ. (See Appendix: A).

This relatively young religion claims to have basic concepts similar to pseudo-Judeo/Christian principles, such as 'only one God' (who created all things) who has one main 'Messiah' (whose teachings are to be adhered to by all mankind) and one hell, which is a place of eternal torment.

Adherents of Islam are called Muslims.

The following is a Muslim quotation and is the basic 'confession' of any individual who claims to be an adherent of Islam.

"I bear witness that there is no god worthy of worship except for the One True God Allah [Who is alone and without any partners] and I bear witness that Muhammad is the Messenger and slave of Allah."

Many Muslims believe and claim that their religion has basically the same roots as that of both Jews and Christians, citing the original Covenant of Abraham recorded in The Book of Genesis (meaning beginnings) as a common denominator.

However, there is also one principal difference found in the Koran (the reputed teachings of Mohammed, the prophet of Islam). That principle difference is discussed later (see pages 44 - 48).

THE KORAN

The Koran is the sacred book of Islam but it was not actually written personally by Mohammed, who was, for all accounts and purposes, an illiterate and uneducated man.

In 632 AD, at the age of 63 years, Mohammed died of fever in Medina. His bones still lie in the tomb where he was buried. Apparently, adherents of Islam wrote the Koran subsequent to this date.

The writings of the Koran, quoted freely throughout this study, are relatively simple, straightforward, easy to understand and demonstrate clearly that Islam especially opposes traditional Judaism, modern Jewish beliefs, Christianity and modern Christian beliefs.

Adherents of Judaism are called Jews.

Most adherents of Judaism, if asked, would specify that they are still awaiting the approach of the long-promised Jewish Messiah, who is yet to arrive someday to bring peace on the earth.

These Jewish adherents are obviously unable to also adhere to teachings from any promised Messiah, which they have not yet received.

Followers of Judaism adhere to the Torah, which contains the writings and roots of the history of the children of Israel and of Judaism.

THE TORAH

The five books of Torah (meaning Law or Teachings) reputedly written by a man called Moses, record, among other things, that G-d created all things and that the name of G-d the Creator is 'YHWH' (Jehovah) or 'I Am'.

The Torah records how G-d chose to make a covenant with a man called Abram.

As part of the covenant, Abram became renamed 'Abraham'.

Apparently the account of creation and of this covenant was kept alive by oral tradition until eventually it was written down by Moses, a well-known Israelite leader.

The famous 'Ten Commandments' were given by G-d to Moses and recorded in the Torah.

According to the original proponents of Judaism, G-d has chosen to reveal Himself to the people of the world solely through writers born amongst the Children of Israel, which fact is hotly disputed by Muslim scholars and by many other religions around the world.

THE TENACH

Other inspired writings were added to the Torah as history (or 'His story') unfolded and collectively these books are called the Tenach, which contains the full 39 books of the Jewish canon, including the Torah (Law), the Naviim (Prophets) and the Kethubim (Writings).

The collective writings of Jewish history became generally known as 'The Bible' (meaning 'The Book') Jewish people are still known today as 'The Chosen People' or 'The People of the Book'. One Jewish lady, reflecting on the constant harassment that has been the lot of the Jews throughout history, once asked me almost bitterly, "Chosen People? – Chosen for what?" I replied that her people were chosen to preserve the Holy Scriptures that contain the veiled explanation of God's Way of Salvation for all mankind. I also explained that being chosen for that purpose did not exclude the Jews from having to personally meet the requirements for receiving God's Y'shua (Salvation) in the same manner as is offered to all the gentile nations. It is reported in the Book of John, Chapter 4 and verse 22, that Y'shua said this,

"Ye worship ye know not what: we know what we worship: for salvation is of the Jews".

THE BIBLE

The Bible is actually a collection of books, reputedly written by Jewish men from various walks of life that were, we understand, inspired by God.

Many adherents of modern Judaism claim that the last divinely inspired book on earth was the book of Malachi, written around 400 BC and the final book of the Tenach. This book ended with an exhortation to 'remember the Law of Moses', together with a promise of 'the coming of the great and dreadful day of the Lord.

Some four hundred years after Malachi, a series of Jewish books and letters of exhortation became accepted as inspired by God and became known collectively as 'The New Testament'.

THE NEW TESTAMENT

There are 27 missives in the canon of the New Testament, which was written by followers and disciples of the Jewish Rabbi, known as Jesus Christ.

The name Jesus means 'Jehovah saves', while the title of Christ means, 'the anointed one'.

Initially, most of those followers (who believed that this man Jesus was the promised Jewish Messiah) were themselves Jewish.

However, since the message brought by Jesus Christ was for 'anyone who would believe', gradually many non-Jews joined the ranks of this innovative Jewish sect.

WHERE DID CHRISTIANS ORIGINATE?

The New Testament refers to Christians as being like wild branches grafted into the roots of the tree of the Covenant Root of the Children of Israel (see page 48 and Romans 11:17).

In time, both the Jewish and non-Jewish believers in Jesus Christ became collectively called 'Christians', meaning 'followers of the Anointed One'.

THIS IS BECAUSE ADHERENTS OF CHRISTIANITY BELIEVE THAT JESUS CHRIST IS THE MESSIAH OF THE JEWS.

The New Testament therefore is a Jewish book and is, in part, a continuation of Israel's history.

Since most adherents of Christianity believe that the Bible is now fully completed by the addition of the New Testament, they reject any 'additions' (such as the writer of the Koran offers).

Most adherents of Christianity therefore generally reject the claims of Islam regarding the supposed inspiration of the Koran by God the Creator.

CHRISTIANITY AND THE
MESSIAH OF THE JEWS

Most adherents of Christianity believe that Jesus Christ fulfilled many Jewish prophecies regarding the coming of the Messiah, promised throughout the Old Testament (i.e. the Tenach).

Most adherents of Christianity believe that Jesus Christ was sired by the Holy Spirit of God, born of a virgin, killed by crucifixion, raised from the dead by God and left the world again with a promise to return to bring a thousand years of lasting peace.

Most Jewish Christians, Christian Zionists, Messianic Jews and Netzarim know the 'Messiah of the Jews' by the Hebraic name of 'Yeshua' or 'Y'shua' (Y'shua means 'YHWH SAVES') sometimes using the Hebraic title, Y'shua Ha Mashiach', which means Y'shua the Messiah.

Others know Him simply as Jesus, the One who offers 'salvation', a descendant of Abraham and, in being a Jew, is a legal recipient of the promises made to Abraham by God.

Most adherents of Christianity believe that, when any person accepts Messiah as his or her Lord by confessing the same, asking for forgiveness of sin and asking the Spirit of Jesus Christ to live within their personal inner being, the promises made to the descendants of Abraham become real and pertinent to that recipient, regardless of previous beliefs, actions, race, age or gender.

Most adherents of Christianity believe that God's offer of 'salvation' through Jesus, is free to anyone, Jew, Arab or otherwise who is willing to accept the offer, to accept Jesus Christ for who He claimed to be and to follow His teachings.

THE EFFECT OF ACCEPTING Y'SHUA AS THE MESSIAH OF THE JEWS

After acceptance, the Jew still remains a Jew (albeit a 'Messianic' Jew) the Arab remains an Arab, but…

No Muslim can remain a Muslim after accepting this offer from Jesus Christ!

Since the writer of the Koran seeks to displace Jesus Christ as the most important person who ever lived, while adding claims of the worth of Mohammed, it is impossible for a Muslim to retain faith in Islam while accepting the claims of Jesus Christ. Though a Jewish Christian will continue to study and believe the Tenach or the 'Old Testament', the ex-Muslim must forsake all the teachings of the Koran.

ISLAM ESPECIALLY OPPOSES MODERN CHRISTIAN BELIEF

Most Muslims deny that Jesus Christ is still alive and that He was the only man to raise Himself from the dead and that He is to return once again as the acclaimed and acknowledged Son of God. Muslims also claim that it was not actually Jesus who died on the cross and that, when he returns he will have to be taught to pray according to the Koran.

ISLAMIC DENIAL OF ALL OF THE
MAJOR CLAIMS OF JESUS CHRIST

Naturally, staunch adherents of Islam deny most of the claims and many of the statements made by Y'shua such as, 'Abraham rejoiced to see my day' and, 'Before Abraham was, I Am'.

On that point some Muslims actually find a common ground with many adherents of Judaism, who also do NOT wish to acknowledge the many claims of Jesus of Nazareth.

It seems though, that most Muslims consider Christianity to be just an extension of original Judaism, seeing as Christians necessarily acknowledge the Messianic line as flowing through Isaac and the Jewish people RATHER than Ishmael and the Arab nations.

Christians are also referred to as 'People of the Book', because they believe and study all the teachings of the Jewish writers of the Bible, which include both the New and the Old Testaments.

Many Christians believe that they have been adopted into the line of David and grafted into the family tree of the Children of Israel through the presence of the Spirit of the perfect Jew, living in their hearts (Romans 11: 11 - 24). Many Christians therefore believe that they can claim, lay hold on and share all the promises that God made to the descendants of Abraham.

Throughout the Bible, Jesus warned that hell existed, explained how to avoid it and also how to receive eternal life through faith in His name.

BORN A JEW

Jesus of Nazareth, born a Jew, taught many new things such as the concept of binding and casting out demons to heal the afflicted.

Jesus, however, made only one stated 'new commandment'.

Jesus said, "This is my commandment; that you love one another, that your joy might be full."

The KORAN on the other hand, gives many commands with clear instructions to the followers of Mohammed concerning those who do not convert to the faith of Islam.

Let us now examine a few of them

Though there are various translations, this Islamic web site contains an accurate account of just one translation and the following quotations are taken from this version.

http://www.hti.umich.edu/k/koran/simple.html

INSTRUCTIONS TO MUSLIMS
ABOUT UNBELIEVERS

* Koran (The Immunity) 9:29 Fight those who do not believe in Allah, nor in the latter day. nor do they prohibit what Allah and his apostle have prohibited, nor follow the *religion of truth, out of those who have been given the Book;.(fight them) till they pay the jiziya (poll tax) in acknowledgement of superiority and they are in a state of subjection.

* 'religion of truth' IN THE KORAN, is referring only to 'Islam'.

Koran (The Immunity) 9:14 Fight them, Allah will punish them by your hands and bring them to disgrace, and assist you against them and heal the hearts of a believing people.

Koran (the Immunity) 9:123 O you who believe! Fight those of the unbelievers who are near to you and let them find in you hardness; and know that Allah is with those who guard.

Koran (Time) 76:4 Surely we have prepared for the unbelievers chains and shackles and a burning fire.

Koran (the Women) 4:76 Those who believe fight in the way of Allah, and those who disbelieve fight in the way of the *Shaitan. Fight therefore against the friends of the Shaitan; surely the strategy of the Shaitan is weak.

*Shaitan =Satan = the 'adversary'

STEP BY STEP INSTRUCTION

Koran (the Accessions) 8:12 Remember Thy Lord inspired the angels (with the message): "I am with you: give firmness to the believers, I will instill terror into the hearts of the unbelievers. Therefore strike off their heads and strike off every fingertip of them.

Here the author of the Koran is giving step by step instruction on how to treat Kafirs (unbelievers) if they refuse to follow Islam.

Islam divided the Arabian society into two tight compartments: Momins and Kafirs.

The word 'Momin' means ' believer in Mohammed and Allah'.

In contrast a 'Kafir' is a non-believer in the teachings of Mohammed and his god Allah.

The Momins did not have to be better men than the Kafirs in terms of character or consciousness.

Momins had only to recite the 'Kalima' (incantation) - "There is no God but Allah and Mohammed is his Prophet". Just by doing that, the 'Momins' became qualified to kill as many Kafirs as they could or pleased, looting and burning their belongings and enslaving their women and children in the process.

WHAT IF GOD IS SAYING A NEW THING?

A Jew may quote Solomon who said, "There is nothing new under the sun," (Ecclesiastes 1:9) but another could easily ask, "Was the book of Ecclesiastes then the last inspired book?"

Someone else asks, "When then did God say He had finished and done with writing?"

If God is saying a new thing, through new writings we shouldn't be stiff-necked or resistant and the dictates of our God-given consciences together with our knowledge of the accepted canon and inner witness should offer some kind of protection, with a drive to do good and to avoid evil.

A Christian quotes Jesus Christ on the cross, who said, "It is finished!" but another asks, "Why then were the gospels and letters written well after that statement?" Another quotes the book of the Revelation of John saying, "If anyone adds to these things, God will add to him the plagues, written in this book and if anyone takes away from the words of this prophecy, God shall take away his part from the Book of Life." (Revelation 22:19, KJV)

Who can deny that none can change any part of that particular prophecy given to John, nor add anything new to the book of Ecclesiastes? Nevertheless, life, commentaries and other writings can continue.

THE ARGUMENT—DIFFERENT AND NEW WRITINGS FROM GOD?

How then are we to judge if any other different and new writings are from God?

There were seven lamps on the top of the seven branches of the Menorah to give light in the Holy place, of the Tabernacle, symbolizing the perfection of the light of the Holy Spirit.

But were there not found sixty-six almond ornaments along the shaft of that Temple Menorah?

The numbers were set and unchangeable, just as is the number of the books.

Surely we should remain open to receive any words that God would write, wherever He chooses to write them, so that, just as Daniel read the writing on the wall, we may understand what God is saying to us or to others.

However, when an otherwise good man gets led astray by deceptive teachings the spirit of pride can attempt to keep his eyes turned away from the admission of Truth.

It can be very difficult to admit error and to say categorically, 'I was wrong—and I WAS DECEIVED'.

"ALLAH WORKS THROUGH HIS PEOPLE"

Koran (the Accessions) 8:17 So you did not slay them, but it was Allah Who slew them, and you did not smite when you smote (the enemy), but it was Allah Who smote, and that He might confer upon the believers a good gift from Himself;

Actually, in this case the writer of the Koran seems to be trying to alleviate the consciences of Muslims who kill others by saying they are not really responsible for such murders because actually it was 'Allah' who was the one who was murdering unbelievers through the hands of fundamentalist Muslims.

This seems similar to the North American comedian who always got a laughing response from his audience by saying, "the Devil made me do it!"

But what do fundamental Muslims fear most? (see page 42 and 43)

> "The spiritual words we speak are as the spiritual sword
> that cuts and is light that cuts through the darkness."

SUBJUGATE AND DEAL RIGOROUSLY WITH THE INFIDEL!

Koran (the Immunity) 9:73 Prophet, strive hard (make war) against the unbelievers and the hypocrites and deal rigorously with them. Hell shall be their Home: an evil fate.

Koran (the women) 4:144 Believers, do not choose the unbelievers rather than the faithful as your friends. Would you give Allah a clear proof against yourselves?

The writer of the Koran, perhaps in order to ensure that Muslims would not get influenced by anyone who might question the validity of his claims, states that if a Muslim befriends a non-Muslim then the wrath of Allah will be on him. Therefore in fundamentalist Islamic sects, people of other religions are treated with contempt, disrespect and cruelty. Muslims are also thus cleverly made to be fearful and afraid of investigating the veracity of any claims suggesting that there could be deception in Islam.

Koran (The Dinner Table) 5:33–34 The punishment of those who make war against Allah and His messenger and strive after corruption in the land will be that they will be murdered or crucified, or their hands and their feet should be cut off on alternate sides. or they should be imprisoned.; this shall be a disgrace for them in this world, and in the hereafter they shall have a grievous chastisement; Save those who repent before ye overpower them. For know that Allah is forgiving, merciful.

In the above verse, the writer of the Koran is once again instructing Muslims in exactly what kind of violence was required for afflicting unbelievers (i.e. all people of other religions or beliefs). Plainly this is not just a judgement of hell to come, but is a terror recommended by the Koran to be inflicted on all 'unbelievers' here and now!

WHO IS AS VILE AS THE UNBELIEVER?

Koran (the Accessions) 8:55 Surely the vilest of animals in Allah's sight are those who disbelieve.

Koran (the Inevitable) 69:31–33 And burn ye him in the blazing fire. Further, make him march in a chain, whereof the length is seventy cubits. This was he that would not believe in Allah Most high.

Through these verses, the Koran, which is treated as a timeless scripture by Muslims, is teaching how lowly unbelievers should be treated by Muslims, regardless of time or space.

Why are fundamentalist Jews and Christians especially abhorrent to fundamentalist Muslims?

The writer of the Koran specifically instructs adherents of Islam to abhor Jews and Christians. (see pages 37-38, 44-46, and 115)

SPECIFIC INSTRUCTIONS TO MUSLIMS REGARDING CHRISTIANS AND JEWS

The writer of the Koran has reserved a special position for certain sects of 'Unbelievers'. Those specially despised 'unbelievers' are none other than followers of Christianity and Judaism.

Koran (the Dinner table) 5:51 Believers, take neither Jews nor Christians for your friends. They are friends with one another. Whoever of you seeks their friendship shall become one of their number. Allah does not guide the wrongdoers.

In that verse the author of the Koran is showing his opinion of Jews and Christians.

Koran (the Dinner table) 5:64 The Jews say: 'Allah's hand is chained.' May their own hands be chained! May they be cursed for what they say!

Remember that many learned Jews do not accept the name of 'Allah' other than as an originally pagan and an idolatrous usurper of the place of reverence reserved for the true G-d of Israel.

Koran (the Immunity) 9:29 Fight those who believe not in Allah nor the latter day, nor hold the forbidden which hath been forbidden by Allah and his messenger, nor follow the Religion of Truth from among the People of the Book, until they pay the Jiziyah with willing submission. And feel themselves subdued.

In the Koran, remember, 'People of the Book' refers to Christians and Jews.

In the Koran, the 'Religion of Truth' refers only to Islam, so in the above verse, the author of the Koran is instructing Muslims to fight Christians and Jews (who necessarily do not believe in his Islamic version of god) until they pay tax to Muslims for their very existence.

Muslims are thus instructed by the Koran writer to make Christians and Jews feel 'subdued'.

Koran (the Immunity) 9:30 The Jews call 'Uzayr-a son of Allah', and the Christians call 'Christ the Son Of Allah'. That is a saying from their mouth; (In this) they but intimate what the unbelievers of old used to say. Allah's curse be on them: how they are deluded away from the Truth.

The author of the Koran is simply moving Muslims to put Allah's curse on all Jews and all Christians.

Note: Since both Jews and Christians commonly accept that Allah is definitely not the true name of God the Creator of all things, understanding that God is called

'YHWH' or 'Jehovah', somewhere in all this is either deception or a deliberate lie.

WHERE MANY FUNDAMENTAL JEWS AND FUNDAMENTAL CHRISTIANS CAN AGREE

From studying Scripture and history, knowledgeable Judeo-Christians have come to the conclusion and understanding that 'Allah' is a demonically-inspired name, derived originally from an ancient pagan deity (see pages 60 and 62) made for the purpose of forcing people into following demonic teachings and violence whilst deceiving them into believing that such demonic teachings are actually from God the Creator.

ISLAMIC HELL AND UNBELIEVERS

Koran (the Clear evidence) 98:6 Surely those who disbelieve from among the People of the Book and the pagans shall burn for ever in the fire of Hell. They are the worst of all men.

Here again, "People of The Book" refers to Christians and Jews. So the author of the Koran is stating categorically that Christians, Jews and pagans are the worst of all men in the world (some translations say 'the vilest of men').

Koran 22:19–22 Garments of fire have been prepared for the unbelievers. Scalding water shall be poured upon their heads, melting their skins and that which is in their bellies.

Here the author of the Koran has imagined vividly how people of other religions should be punished in hell. It seems he is trying to make sure that people of other religions convert to Islam out of sheer terror of hell. And if this terror doesn't work, then the Muslims are instructed to convert unbelievers to Islam brutally (and by force) in 'Jihad'.

Throughout the text of the KORAN there appears to be continuously repeated exhortations to use force and terror to make converts to Islam.

CAN ANY MUSLIM CLAIM DIFFERENTLY?

Ask your Muslim friends to explain the above Koran verses otherwise!

Because in the Koran, both Jews and Christians are referred to as "The People of The Book", there is a question that logically follows that understanding.

THE GOD OF THE JEWS IS THE GOD OF ABRAHAM.

How is it possible to love and obey the God of Israel, while simultaneously hating the Jews?

In 'The Book', this same God promised Abraham that He would' make a great nation out of him'. God is also recorded in Genesis as having said to Abraham, "I will bless those who bless you and curse him that curses you, and in you shall all families of the earth be blessed".

WHAT IS THE BLESSING OF ABRAHAM, AND THROUGH WHICH NATION DOES IT COME?

What kind of blessing are we receiving from this 'great nation', promised by God?

We understand from the Bible that the blessings from God are to come through connecting ourselves with the promised Messiah who comes from that great nation as promised by God.

THIS MESSIAH COMES FROM WHICH GREAT NATION?

From Abraham's sons, Ishmael and Isaac, came two separate nations.

One group believes that Ishmael's nation was the nation of blessing, while another group believes that Isaac's nation was the one referred to by God.

One of these groups must therefore be walking in either error or deception!

Who is the deceiver, but Satan the destroyer? (see page 78)

So, one must ask oneself, which group is in error, or

being deceived and which one is practicing the works of his father?

Most adherents of Christianity believe that the Messiah is Jesus Christ, the Lion of the Tribe of Judah, who rose from the dead and left the earth with a promise to return.

Christians therefore necessarily believe that the nation of the man called Israel, who was born as Jacob the son of Isaac, is the nation that God chose to use to bless all the families of the earth.

Most adherents of Christianity can believe this because the Torah records that God told Jacob that "in his seed all the families of the earth would be blessed".

WHO IS THE SEED?

This 'Seed' refers to the Messiah of Israel, who was to come.

According to 'The Book', they believe that the God of Israel was to manifest Himself in the flesh (as a man) as it is written in the book of the prophet Isaiah;

"For unto us a child is born; unto us a son is given; and the government shall be upon His shoulder and His name shall be called Wonderful, Counselor, The mighty God, The everlasting Father, the Prince of Peace". Isaiah9:6 (Yeshayah 9:6)

"Face truth, accept truth, become one with truth, move with truth—and truth will set us free!"

THE JEWISH VIEWPOINT

Most Jewish people are taught by rabbis to expect the promised Messiah to make a first time appearance as an entirely different person than the Jesus that fundamental Christians wait for.

This event, the rabbis believe, will prove once and for all, that Jewish resistance was right all along to reject the offer of Y'shua (meaning YHWH is salvation) who died on the cross of Calvary.

FIGHTING AGAINST
SATANIC DECEPTION

Koran (the Women) 4:76 Those who believe fight in the way of Allah, and those who disbelieve fight in the way of the *Shaitan. Fight therefore against the friends of the Shaitan; surely the strategy of the Shaitan is weak. (*Shaitan =Satan = the 'adversary').

By deceiving many into believing that the nation from Abraham's other son was the real recipient of the promise, Satan has produced an army of destruction to fight against God's promised blessings.

THE REALLY IMPORTANT QUESTION
IS THIS: "WHICH SON?"

"Which son was the promised blessing to come through?"

Satan was always proud of his destructive power, which was his necessary downfall (see page 78).

When Y'shua spoke to certain religious leaders and rebuked them for manifesting the works of "their father, the Devil", they became furious.

It seems obvious that those who choose Satan for a 'father', will then try to destroy others along with themselves, according to the nature of their father.

Can this be called a blessing or shall we say, 'By their fruits we shall know them'?

THE SATANIC DECEPTION VIEWPOINT

The teachings of the G-d of Israel in the Torah and the teachings of the writer of the Koran have several things in common (One God, one main Messiah or Prophet, one hell, etc.) and it seems that one is trying to imitate the other.

Can one be true and the other false? Indeed, must one be true and the other false?

Is one of these religions actually a religion created by Satan to twist the message of the other and to deceive any possible seekers of truth before they find it? Who is Satan? (See pages 58, 94, 97, 99 100 and 129)

WESTERN UNDERSTANDING

To the western mind, the Koran may seem to be filled with hate and threatening throughout, with very little that is really spiritual but what if we try to understand the spirit behind the Koran?

The entire reward for being a devout Muslim man is seemingly described by fundamental Islamic sects as an eternity of rivers of wine and sex with supernatural Houris.

To many in the West who have not yet accepted such Islamic teachings, the Koran seems to be an instruction manual encouraging murder, looting, terrorists, bigots, tyrants, and oppressors.

But, perhaps western people just do not understand this type of 'spirituality'.

Then again, are 'peaceful Muslims' even aware of these verses?

Or are peaceful Muslims, like so many followers in other religions, just 'blissfully unaware' of what their religious book actually teaches?

In other words, have 'peaceful Muslims' even read their own book?

ARE THERE ANY TRULY PEACEFUL MUSLIMS?

Do not forget that many individuals who would still call themselves 'Muslim' have fled from Muslim-controlled oppression.

Like a lot of Christians and Jews, who do not really know what their Scripture says, many Muslims have not even read all that their 'holy book' actually says, so many may have not even considered the possibility that their teachers could have been deceived!

Many are not even truly aware of the 'teachings of hate' exposed by this writing and who has the right to criticize the Bible or the Koran unless they have first at least checked out the contents?

TWO TYPES OF BELIEVERS

There appear to be two types of believers common to Muslims, Christians and Jews.

Those who have studied their holy book/s, who understand why they believe what they believe and why they conduct themselves in the manner of their faith.

Those who have not studied their holy book/s and therefore do not exactly understand why they say they believe what they believe or why they conduct themselves in a certain manner.

GIVING PEACEFUL MUSLIMS, CHRISTIANS AND JEWS THE BENEFIT OF THE DOUBT

Firstly, perhaps we should give peaceful Muslims the benefit of the doubt and simply ask them to explain why they believe as they do.

For example, did 'peaceful Muslims' just accept the Islamic faith blindly or through tradition handed down or even out of fear, or is there some other explanation?

Perhaps some Muslims, Christians and Jews are just apathetic and have not truly 'thought it all through'.

If any Muslim reads the foregoing list of actual 'teachings of Mohammed', taken from the Koran, they would have to admit that, as Muslims, they are being instructed and required to hate, fight and kill those who do not agree with the teachings of the writer of the Koran.

Many so-called 'Muslims' would not agree with such teachings to use force on non-Muslims to maim and to kill. Why then do they still call themselves 'Muslims'? - Ask them.

Are peaceful Muslims deceived or not? Are Jews and Christians deceived?

Are non-Muslims deceived?—Are they deceived or are non-Muslims deceived?

WHO IS DECEIVED?

Which group is not willing to have their established values and doctrines logically examined?

Individuals from which group become satanically violent when their instilled belief-system and values are questioned?

Which group is ignoring the well-established and provable facts of history, archaeology and the light of day?

Surely any reader should think for himself or herself, using open logic and an honest desire for Truth. Can we not all agree with this statement? "Let's all get in step with the truth of God!"

TRUTH IS TRUTH BUT WHO IS WILLING TO HONESTLY SEARCH IT OUT?

It is said that a man who believes a lie has been fooled, but a man who willingly lies to himself and then believes the lie is more than twice a fool and a liar.

Wishfulness is not truth and one who wishes that the Truth of life were not so, leaves an open door for the liar to make of him a twice-dead fool.

ISLAM IS A TERRITORIAL RELIGION AND DIVIDES THE WORLD INTO TWO BASIC CAMPS

1. "Dar al-Islam" [House of Islam] consists of all lands where Islam has prevailed at any time.
2. "Dar al-Harb" [House of War] is all other unconquered lands where jihad must eventually be waged.

The fundamentalist teaching of the KORAN is that it is the duty of every able Muslim to join the holy struggle to win back, through force of arms, all territories that Islam had at one time conquered that have been lost over the centuries. This includes present-day Israel, the Iberian Peninsula [Spain and Portugal], and large parts of southeastern Europe up to Vienna.

AFTER THAT—THE WORLD!

The whole world?—Is Islam intent on forcing Islamic rules upon everyone in the world?

Yes indeed, the fundamentalist Muslims also promote the ideal of a promised renewed golden age of Islam, when the faith of Mohammed will rule the entire world.

Do Muslim regimes similar to the infamous Taliban envision themselves as eventually governing the nations as part of this leadership?

They most certainly do!!

THE LONG-AWAITED CALIPH

'Caliph' is an Islamic concept, almost the equivalent of the Jewish and Christian 'Messiah', but perhaps more perfectly aligned with the old German political concept of Das Fuehrer (the Leader).

Many Muslims await a modern-day pan-Islamic figure—a new 'caliph'—to lead this physical battle against 'the infidel' nations. It appears that the late Khomeini, Saddam Hussein, bin Laden, and even Arafat have aspired to claim this mantle at various times by their decrees of jihad against their respective enemies and territories.

This is the Islamic Caliph of Jihad, as opposed to the peaceful Messiah awaited by the Christian and the Jew alike of whom it is written, in their common Scriptures,

"Of the increase of His government and peace there shall be no end upon the throne of David and upon His kingdom to order it and to establish it with judgement and with justice from henceforth even for ever. The zeal of the Lord of Hosts will perform this."

Isaiah 9:7 (Yeshayah 9:7)

"DEATH TO THE INFIDELS!"

This common agenda has been aided of late by a series of fatwas, or religious decrees, by leading Muslim clerics. Among other things, these fatwas declare that suicide attacks are an acceptable form of jihad; that the US is an appropriate target for assaults, and, in a very recent ruling, that any Muslim who cooperates with non-Muslim intelligence agencies is an apostate worthy of death.

Militant Muslim leaders view America as the main impediment to their quest to spread Islam throughout the entire world through jihad and thus, the US is widely presented by Muslim clerics as the "Great Satan" which must be defeated in battle.

Text of Fatwah Urging Jihad Against Americans Published in Al-Quds al-'Arabi on Febuary 23, 1998 AD (http://www.ict.org.il/articles/fatwah.htm)

Satan, remember, is an angelic being/person with a fallen nature and having control of an invisible army of fallen angels/demonic spirits who are co-existent with mankind living here on this earth. Satan is an actually existent and an absolutely real spiritual being and he is not a nation or a religion, but his influence on the minds of his 'puppets' is more readily seen in politics, crime, corruption, sin and false religions in every part of the world.

Satan seems to have had a certain measure of success and we can see by looking around that he still takes delight in enslaving mankind through a variety of religions and false belief systems.

SATAN AND HIS
SPIRITUAL PRINCIPALITIES
ARE THE REAL ENEMY!

The question that arises here is "But how do you fight a spiritual enemy that is unseen and who attacks you through your friends, in attempting to influence neighbors, strangers and even your brothers and family members against you?" (See page 102).

THE ROOTS OF TRUE AND
FALSE RELIGIONS

Scholars throughout the years have traced back the roots of religion and find two basic sources, where beliefs have sprouted to form what we call 'religion'.

1. Israel and district: Judeo-Christian belief, founded on the historical details and principles found in the Book of Books known collectively as 'the Bible'.
2. Iraq and area: According to a summation of said scholar's reports, found in the late Alexander Hislop's book The Two Babylons, every religion (other than Judeo-Christian) can be traced back to Iraq in the area known then as 'Babylon'. Babylon means 'confusion'. This is actually all recorded in the Bible.

WHICH RELIGION WAS FIRST?

The first 'false religion', seems to have started in Babylon, apparently focused on the deities named Baal and Tammuz (representative of the sun god and the moon god respectively).

As this religion spread throughout the world it changed and evolved, introducing a host of other spiritual beings as so-called gods and goddesses.

Idols were often fashioned in the image of these so-called deities and were reproduced by craftsmen. Increasingly, these images or idols became the subject of worship in the various cults and beliefs that evolved with varying degrees of acceptance.

Large cultures with good communication usually formed agreement on which idol or idols were to be given veneration in their area. In nomad cultures such as the Arab nations, it was common to find each tribe to have its' own specific idol or 'deity'.

In modern India, idolatry has spread so much that today, literally millions of different idols and 'household gods with their demon-spirit attachments' are still being venerated!

POLITICAL EXPEDIENCIES

In ancient times, when a community became settled and communication improved, often rulers tried to stop squabbling over differences of opinion by imposing their own favorite idol or deity to bring the area into religious unity of purpose. This helped to establish a common belief system for political expediency and whether it was true or not may have been considered irrelevant.

In other cases, specific individuals such as Mohammed have separated themselves by claiming to have special spiritual knowledge or revelation and have adapted their country's belief systems to what they felt was a more perfect way.

These are the religions of old, rooted in 'Babylon', which tradition and habitual adherence have been kept alive to this very day.

NAMES OF THE MOON GOD

The names given by men to the moon god varied from area to area. Nanna, Suen and Assimbabbar were utilized in ancient Sumeria. In Assyria and Babylon, Suen became pronounced 'Sin' as the favorite name for the deity of these moon-cult followers.

Represented by a crescent moon, the god 'Sin' was considered to be the 'controller of the night' or the 'ruler of the darkness'.

THE TITLE OF SIN

The title of the god Sin was 'Al-ilah', which in Arabic means 'the great god', as Al-ilah was considered to be the greatest of all of these pagan gods. These pagans believed that Al-ilah was married to the sun goddess and that the stars were their daughters.

(http://www.biblebelievers.org.au/moongod.htm)

During their time of sojourning in the 'wilderness of Sin', the Israelites, time and time again, were warned by the G-d of Moses never to submit to this particular idolatrous pagan deity being offered by all the neighboring pagan nations. This is recorded in the book of Exodus.

The Israelites were commanded to worship the actual Creator of all things who had revealed Himself to Moses, who had called Himself 'I AM' and whom they knew also as 'YHWH'.

In those days they knew very well that the moon god was not the same entity as the G-d of Israel who had befriended and cut covenant with their forefather Abraham.

THE BIRTH OF ISLAM

In Saudi-Arabia, in the seventh century AD, much of the idol-worship had advanced into veneration of individual tribal gods, kept jealously separate and thus perpetrating division throughout the mostly nomadic tribes of the Arabic world.

THE GODS OF THE QURAYSH TRIBE

Mohammed's family was of the powerful Quraysh (or Kuraysh) tribe, keeper of the Ka'bah, who worshipped a pantheon (or god system) of pagan gods. The greatest of these pagan gods was al-Ilah (Allah or al-Llah) who had three daughters named al-Uzza, Manah, and Allat.

The Quraysh tribe initially, and violently, resisted Mohammaed, Islam, and his followers. They were eventually defeated by the Muslims at the battle of Badr. Then, in the year 630 A.D., the Muslims entered Mecca and destroyed all the other idols (reputedly 167 in total) in the Ka'bah.

Once Mohammed became successful in promoting his pseudo "mono-theism" he decreed that all the other idols and all other forms of pagan worship be banned. Mohammed claimed that Allah, the greatest of their pagan gods, was the same God as the God of the people of the Book, the Hebrews and the Christians. Being encouraged and no doubt influenced by Khadijah, his Catholic wife, he probably even sincerely believed this. If that assumption was correct he deduced that Allah the familiar god (of his father) which had been worshipped for generations by his ancestors must be the actual creator of all things. Mohammed now began to insist that his god alone be worshipped and, after some initial and bloody resistance, this new "monotheistic" religion brought some degree of religious unity to the Arab world. The last local group to succumb was a military alliance led by the Thaqif Tribe from the mountain city of Taif.

The Arabs of the Thaqif Tribe all worshipped the goddess "Al-ilat" (Allat) the daughter of Allah. Considered the most powerful of all the deities worshipped by pagans in those days, Allat continued to be venerated alongside Al-Llah until the Thaqif tribe and their allies were finally subdued and forced to embrace Islam and Allah alone.

THE ORIGIN OF THE FLAG OF ISLAM

The crescent moon and the stars, originally symbolic of the moon god and his daughter goddesses, were retained on the flag of this new religion and are still the symbol of Islam today, linked with the spreading of the Islamic belief system in all continents of the earth, while their origins are either ignored or rationalized as irrelevant.

JEWS, CHRISTIANS AND MUSLIMS ALL AGREE ON AT LEAST ONE THING—TO A POINT!

Though all three of these religious groups agree and admit that the Creator of all things spoke to Abraham and commanded him to sacrifice his son as a test of faith and obedience, there is a related point where differing opinions clash head-on with historic truth and logical thinking.

If God is love, which 'religions' teach love?

Which religion was first?

Which religion is imitating the other but adding satanic lies?

They cannot all be true!

THE DIFFERENCE OF
OPINION BEGINS HERE.

Abraham had two sons. Only one of them could be the ancestor of God's blessing to the world.

The elder son was called Ishmael, whom Abraham had sired with his wife's bondmaid Hagar.

The younger son was called Isaac and was born to Abraham's wife Sarah.

Ishmael became the father of the twelve Arab nations.

Isaac became the father of twins whom he named Esau and Jacob.

Esau had appeared as firstborn but his brother had emerged grasping the heel of the 'elder' so the second born was therefore called Jacob (meaning 'the supplanter').

Later in life, in a moment of weakness, the first born sold his birthright to his younger brother Jacob. This was a cause of strife between them and, in the grace and purposes of God, Jacob was removed to a distant part of the country for a set number of years.

Jacob later had a dream in which the Lord spoke clearly identifying Himself as the God of Abraham and the God of Isaac.

The Lord promised to bless all the families of the earth through the Seed of Jacob.

Jacob called the place by the name of Beth-el, meaning 'House of God' and made a vow to serve God and to give back a tenth of all that God would give to him.

JACOB BECOMES ISRAEL.

Jacob ended up with two wives who had each lent their respective handmaidens to him so that he had sired eleven sons by the time he returned to meet his brother Esau.

On that journey, Jacob saw angels at the place called Mahanaim (meaning two armies). Later, Jacob had his time of wrestling at a place he called Peni-el (meaning face of God) where he was told he would be called no more Jacob (meaning supplanter) but instead he would be called 'Israel' (meaning 'he shall be prince of God').

After making peace with his brother Esau, Israel purchased land next to the city of Shalem and spread his tent there.

Shalem, in those days, had the meaning 'at peace, safe, complete and perfect' and is now called Jerusalem, which today is still referred to as the City of Peace.

In that place Israel erected an altar and called it El-elohe-Israel (meaning God, the God of Israel).

Thus Abraham became the father of all the Israelite tribes, including the tribe of Judah which has lent its name to all descendents of Israel who are also now called 'the Jews' and are thus recipients of all the promises made to Abraham by God the Creator.

Abraham is therefore the father of all the Arab nations through Ishmael the elder and also of all the Jewish peoples through Isaac the younger.

WHY WOULD BROTHER FIGHT AGAINST BROTHER?

The Promises were given to Abraham's descendants through only one of his sons.

The Islamic religion was founded on the concept that the son offered by Abraham for sacrifice was Ishmael, the father of the Arabs, while the Jews believe that the son offered for sacrifice by Abraham was in fact Isaac, the father of the children of Israel.

Only one of these beliefs can be based on the true account as recorded in the Holy Scriptures.

Ancient copies of the Scriptures dating back many hundreds of years have been found in the area of the Dead Sea and these ancient copies confirmed the following account of the covenant that God the Creator made with Abraham.

The following account is taken directly from several relevant passages of the Authorised Version of the King James Translation of the Holy Scriptures.

THE COVENANT THAT GOD THE
CREATOR MADE WITH ABRAHAM.

Genesis 22:

> Now it came to pass after these things that God tested Abraham, and said to him "Abraham!" And he said "Here I am."

> And He said, "take now your son, your only son Isaac, whom you love, and go to the land of Moriah, and offer him there as a burnt offering on one of the mountains of which I shall tell you."

> So Abraham rose early in the morning and saddled his donkey, and took two of his young men with him, and Isaac his son: and he split the wood for the burnt offering and arose and went to the place of which God had told him.

> Then on the third day Abraham lifted his eyes and saw the place afar off.

> And Abraham said to his young men, "Stay here with the donkey; the lad and I will go yonder and worship, and we will come back to you."

> So Abraham took the wood of the burnt offering and laid it on Isaac his son; and he took the fire in his hand, and a knife, and the two of them went together.

But Isaac spoke to Abraham his Father and said, "My father!" And he said, "Here I am, my son." And he said, "Look, the fire and the wood, but where is the lamb for a burnt offering?"

And Abraham said, "My son, God will provide Himself the lamb for a burnt offering." And the two of them went together.

Then they came to the place of which God had told him. And Abraham built an altar of wood in order; and he bound Isaac his son and laid him on the altar, upon the wood.

And Abraham stretched out his hand and took the knife to slay his son.

But the angel of the Lord called to him from Heaven and said, "Abraham, Abraham!" And he said, "Here I am."

And He said, "Do not lay your hand on the lad, or do anything to him; for now I know that you fear God, since you have not withheld your son, your only son, from me."

Then Abraham lifted his eyes and looked, and there behind him was a ram caught in a thicket by its horns. So Abraham went and took the ram and offered it up for a burnt offering instead of his son.

And Abraham called the name of the place, 'The Lord will provide'; as it is said to this day, "In the Mount of the Lord it shall be provided."

Then the Angel of the Lord called to Abraham a second time out of heaven,

And said: "By Myself I have sworn, says the Lord, because you have done this thing, and have not withheld your son, your only son,

"in blessing I will bless you, and in multiplying I will multiply your descendants as the stars of the heaven and as the sand that is on the sea shore; and your descendants shall possess the gates of their enemies".

AUTHOR'S NOTE:

The scientists tell us that there are more stars in the universe than there are grains of sand on all the beaches in the world, but who shall possess the gates of hell?

BLESSINGS ARE PROMISED TO ALL NATIONS OF EARTH THROUGH THE SEED OF ABRAHAM!

Genesis 22 (continued)

"In your seed all the nations of the earth shall be blessed, because you have obeyed My voice."

In a previous chapter of the Holy Bible, the events leading up to this event are described as follows.

Genesis 17: Verses 1 - 9

When Abram was ninety-nine years old, the Lord appeared to Abram and said to him, "I am Almighty God; walk before Me and be blameless.

"And I will make my covenant between Me and you, and will multiply you exceedingly."

Then Abram fell on his face, and God talked with him, saying;

"As for Me, behold My covenant is with you, and you shall be a father of many nations.

"No longer shall your name be called Abram, but your name shall be Abraham: for I have made you a father of many nations.

"I will make you exceedingly fruitful: and I will make nations of you and kings shall come from you.

"Also I give to you and your descendants after you in their generations, for an everlasting covenant, to be God to you and your descendants after you.

"Also I give to you and your descendants after you the land in which you are a stranger, all the land of Canaan, as an everlasting possession; and I will be their God."

"And God said to Abraham: "As for you, you shall keep My covenant, you and your descendants after you throughout their generations.

Genesis 17: Verses18 - 21

And Abraham said to God, "Oh, that Ishmael might live before you!"

Then God said: "No, Sarah your wife shall bear you a son, and you shall call his name Isaac: I will establish My covenant with him for an everlasting covenant, and with his descendants after him.

"And as for Ishmael, I have heard you. Behold, I have blessed him, and will make him fruitful, and will multiply him exceedingly. He shall beget twelve princes, and I will make him a great nation.

"But My covenant I will establish with Isaac, whom Sarah shall bear to you at this set time next year."

So the line of Isaac, the ancestor of Israel, was the one through whom the promise would come.

But when He returns, will He find faith on the earth? So asked the Prince of princes, who was aforementioned in the prophetic words of Daniel.

THAT ORIGINAL COVENANT
WAS MADE WITH ABRAHAM
BY ALMIGHTY GOD

That original covenant, to be established through Isaac, was made for the benefit of all mankind, which benefit Satan constantly tries to hinder, by causing man to fight against man instead of against his own evil intentions.

The Scriptures say that Abraham's faith was accounted to him for righteousness.

We know that faith is the substance of things hoped for and the evidence for things not seen, but do we not consider logic, seeing as God has given us minds to reason with?

IS THERE NOT A PLACE FOR
LOGIC IN ALL THIS?

There surely is a place for logic in all this disputing.

If almighty God created and predestined mankind to have a relationship with Him, similar to the relationship that a dependent wife has with her husband, do you think that He would allow anyone to rob Him of His goal?

If God views the earth as a field in which He has planted a crop which is to be harvested in order to populate His heavenly realms for His fellowship and His pleasure, do you think that any created being could ever frustrate His plan?

When God said, "Not by might, not by power, but by

My Spirit," do you not think He has a plan outside of the wars that men have with each other?

What father would want his very own children to fight one another and if God is the Father of the righteous, would He not choose to show a good example to His off-spring on how to behave?

EXAMPLES OF JEWISH PRAYERS THAT ASK FOR PEACE

"May there be abundant peace from heaven, and life for us and for all Israel; and say ye, Amen.

"May He who establishes peace in the heavens, grant peace unto us and unto all Israel; and say ye, Amen."

"Eternal God, who sendest consolation unto all sorrowing hearts, we turn to Thee for solace in this, our trying hour. Though bowed in grief at the passing of our loved ones, we affirm our faith in Thee, our Father, who art just and merciful, who healest broken hearts and art ever near to those who are afflicted. May the Kaddish prayer, proclaiming Israel's hope for Thy true kingdom here on earth, impel us to help speed that day when peace shall be established through justice, and all men recognize their brotherhood in Thee. With trust in Thy great goodness, we who mourn, rise to sanctify Thy name."

PEACE OVER ISRAEL AND OVER ALL THE PEOPLES OF THE EARTH - A JEWISH PRAYER

"O beneficent Father, as we recall this day the gratitude of the children of Israel for the harvest of their fields in Eretz Yisrael [the land of Israel], we, too, acknowledge Thee, the source of all our bounties. For all our blessings we give Thee thanks. May the portion of the Torah we read today teach us to share Thy gifts with those in need. Hasten that day when the children of Israel, in the land of their fathers, shall bring in their sheaves with rejoicing. We pray that Thou, who didst protect our forefathers when they dwelt in tabernacles in the wilderness, will extend Thy tabernacle Amen."

BUT LOGICALLY, WOULD GOD NOT REWARD GOOD BEHAVIOUR?

One would reason that God would reward good behaviour, while correcting and showing disapproval of bad behaviour.

LOGICAL QUESTIONS FOUND IN THE ARABIC NEWS MEDIA

Tunisian columnist Al-'Afif Al-Akhdhar wrote in Al-Hayat, an Arabic daily based in London that it is time for the Arab world to stop blaming others for the various defeats continually handed out to it since Napoleon.

He lays the blame for the failure of the Arab-Israeli peace process squarely at the feet of PLO chief Yasser Arafat.

"After every defeat, we became less courageous in asking [ourselves] painful questions, and more deeply mired in the culture of finding excuses, placing responsibility for our defeats on the unknown and settling for complaining about the trap laid by the West and its 'stepdaughter' Israel," wrote Al-Akhdhar. "All this [has happened] without us asking [ourselves] the embarrassing question of whether internal factors have made us, unlike all other nations, easy prey to all. The [Arab] elites have opted for…denying their overwhelming responsibility for these defeats."

He also wrote: "[Former US President Bill] Clinton presented proposals to the Palestinian leaders on a golden platter, and they answered him with an Intifada of armed struggle and suicide bombings—in an era when these are no longer appropriate. Thus, at one blow, we lost [both] the land…and our reputation. The occupation army returned [to the territories] and in everyone's eyes our image was tarnished by egotism unprecedented in our history."

International Christian Embassy Jerusalem PO Box 1192, Jerusalem, 91010, Israel

IS THERE ANY GOD GREATER
THAN ALLAH?

Perhaps columnist Al-'Afif Al-Akhdhar and others need to truly ask themselves the question, "If Allah is not giving Islam the victory, is there any God greater than Allah?" (see page 82)

BUT, WHY WOULD GOD
BECOME A MAN JUST TO ALLOW
HIMSELF TO BE SACRIFICED?

Could it be that He did this in order that forgiveness might be granted to all that accept and believe, so that all may live for God? All have sinned and therefore all are guilty of that particular murder and all were a part of the cause, but has He not made a way for all to be forgiven?

THINK FOR YOURSELF.

Why did Y'shua say, "In the multitude of the Book, it is written of Me" and why is Y'shua known as 'The Lamb of God'?

Was Jesus not foreshadowed by the lamb provided by God Himself to Abraham in substitute for the son of Sarah?

Submitting to the will of his father, Isaac in a 'type', walked up the hill, carrying the wood that was to be used in his own sacrifice. Later, in a fulfillment of this 'type',

Y'shua submitted to the will of His Father in walking to the Hill, carrying the wooden cross that was used to sacrifice Him as the Lamb of God.

Someone says "The death of Jesus Christ was not a sacrifice, because Jesus was murdered by the Romans and by His brethren the Jews," but I say to you that if any man has sinned in any way he is himself guilty of the blood necessarily shed by God for the redemption of the children of men.

ARE JEWS THEN TO BE EXCLUDED?

Au contraire! According to the New Testament, "Salvation is of the Jews!"

The Jewish Rabbi Paul asked rhetorically, "Has God cast away His people? God forbid! For I also am an Israelite, of the seed of Abraham", so we see that neither the Jews nor the Arabs are excluded from the grace and mercy of God. Can we not praise God for that abounding grace?

If we believe the New Testament Scriptures, we can thank God that we need only to admit our guilt and to ask for forgiveness in the Name of Jesus, the epitome of the perfect Jew, by the grace of God. Ah, the grace and wisdom of our God!

Christians thank God that none has any right to boast so that no one has any excuse for falling by the snare of pride that took Lucifer and robbed him of his position of prominence with God.

We understand from the Scriptures that Lucifer, the

highest of angels and later to be the greatest of the fallen 'gods', became lifted up with pride, which brought about his downfall so that he is now become known as Satan (meaning 'Adversary')—the adversary of the People of the Book!

PRIDE GOES BEFORE A FALL

Pride goes before a fall, but we all must follow the example of the humility and the obedience of Y'shua Ha Mashiach if we want to please God the Creator without falling into the snare of Satan. Obedience is better than sacrifice and Abraham obeyed God.

The substitutional sacrifice of the ram for Abraham's son, Isaac took place on a hill; just as, on the hill of Golgotha the Lamb of God was crucified as a substitute for each of us.

That ram, being caught by its horns in a thorn bush, depicted, in spiritual analogy, the thorns that would be used to make the crown of thorns that pierced the head of the Lord of glory.

The thorns of the crown that pierced the head of the Lord of glory depict the thoughts that Satan has used throughout the ages to attack the minds of the children of men.

Just as Isaac was the only son of Abraham, born to his wife Sarah, Jesus Christ was the only begotten Son of God.

As Isaac, the only legitimate son of Abraham, was

bound upon the wood of the altar, likewise was Y'shua the Messiah, the Lamb of God affixed by nails to the wood of the cross.

AS ISAIAH (YESHAYAH) PROPHESIED.

"He was wounded for our transgressions; He was bruised for our iniquities, The chastisement for our peace was upon Him and by His stripes we are healed. All we, like sheep, have gone astray; we have turned, every one to his own way; And the Lord has laid on Him the iniquity of us all." Isaiah 53: 5–6

SPIRITUAL LANGUAGE

Does God not fulfil our instruction with the use of many allegories?

Spiritual language is often allegorical so, just as dreams and visions can be allegorical, God, Who is Spirit, chooses to use this spiritual means of communication until we are fully matured and adapted to His nature, which is the nature of our Lord Jesus Christ the man. We may choose to see or choose to remain blind to the pictures presented by God who has given us the free will to follow whichever nature we choose to believe. Who can discover the mysteries of the Word?

"He that eateth my flesh, and drinketh my blood, dwelleth in me, and I in him". John 6:56 Why was the Word laid in a 'manger'? How can one eat the flesh of the

Word? How was the Word 'made flesh'? 'Manger comes from the French, meaning 'to eat'. Do we not eat to gain sustenance? How can one grow spiritually except by ingesting the milk and the meat of the Word that gives us life in Him? In whom shall the Nature of the Word that is in Jesus Christ manifest?

"Wherewithal shall a young man cleanse his way? by taking heed thereto according to thy word. With my whole heart have I sought thee: O let me not wander from thy commandments. Thy word have I hid in mine heart, that I might not sin against thee." Psalm 119: 9–11

SYMBOLIC SUBSTITUTION IS A SPIRITUAL LANGUAGE

The spiritual meaning of the pictorial substitution of the ram for the son is obvious to those who choose to look, to see, to understand and to believe!

Blessed be the Lord God who provided Himself a substitute sacrifice in our place!

God created mankind and put them on the earth like a gardener who puts seed into the earth hoping that it will grow but Satan is like an enemy of the gardener, sowing tares to hinder the crop, hoping that the harvest would fail.

The Parable of the Word is seen in the harvest. Just as when stalks of wheat are ready to harvest, the weight of the heads causes them to bow, so do the righteous bow before the Truth! Tares and weeds grow up with the good crop but, unlike the wheat, they refuse to bow to Truth!

A Roman ruler once asked, "What is Truth?"

Who said, 'I am the Way, the Truth and the Life!'?

Who said, 'No man comes to the Father but by me!'?

Who has ascended up into heaven?

Who has gathered the wind in His fists?

Who has bound the waters in a garment?

Who has established all the ends of the earth?

What is His name?

And what is His Son's name if you can tell?…Proverbs 30:4 (Mishlei 30:4)

WHO HAS DARED TO DEFY THE SON?

Who dares to attempt to destroy the Brethren of the Son? Who are the Brethren of the Son?

Our mutual enemy is Satan, the perpetrator of our tendency to self-destruction. (see pages 58, 94, 97, 99, 100 and 129)

Our mutual friend is Abraham, the friend of God, Who gave us the prophesied Seed of Jacob.

He who allows himself to be deceived by the spirit of Satan is not wise, for Satan demands submission with the blood of your children but God has given us His only Son instead!

TRUTH IS SELF-EXISTENT, BUT WISHFUL JEALOUSY CAN LEAD A MAN ASTRAY

Dear reader, have you personally examined and chosen only Truth? Can you, truly say with me, "I have chosen to believe the Truth, no matter what it costs or what it may be, of the One who is the Nature of the Truth, pleasing to God, to His loved ones and to myself as one with them?"

SPIRITUAL PRINCIPLES AND SPIRITUAL TERMINOLOGY: - THE SYMBOLISM EXPLAINED

In the New Testament, in the book of Galatians, written by a Pharisee and Jew of letters, called Saul of Tarsus (known also as Paul), the symbolism of these events is explained in this way.

> For it is written that Abraham had two sons: the one by a bondwoman, the other by a free woman.
>
> But he who was of the bondwoman was born according to the flesh, and he of the free woman through promise.
>
> Which things are symbolic. For these are the two covenants:
>
> the one from Mount Sinai which gives birth to bondage, which is Hagar-

For this Hagar is Mount Sinai in Arabia, and corresponds to Jerusalem which now is, and now is in bondage with her children-

But the Jerusalem above is free, which is the mother of us all.

For it is written:

"Rejoice, o barren, you who do not bear! Break forth and shout, you who do not travail! For the desolate has many more children than she who has a husband"

Now we, brethren, as Isaac was, are children of promise.

But, as he who was born according to the flesh then persecuted him who was born according to the Spirit, even so it is now.

Galations Chapter 4

The present fleshly warfare is not from God the Creator who loves all His creatures.

This scenario of God and His friend Abraham, the ancestor of both the Jews and the Arabs was portrayed as a symbolism depicting the One that was to come as a substitute for their blood.

The ram was the substitute for Isaac. The Lamb of God is the substitute for the believer.

Isaac was spared by God, just as we are spared when we personally accept the Lamb of God.

Seeing that we know God is Spirit, should we be surprised when He teaches us spiritual principles using spiritual terminology?

Pictures, representations and symbols of the promised realm of perfection are utilized throughout the Books of the Book, in order to teach us to think and to communicate in a spiritual manner.

THE COVENANT OF ABRAHAM, THE HANDSHAKE OF GOD

So the Word teaches, reaching out for your heart to grasp as in the handshake of a friend of God. This you become when you trust, acknowledge and cling to the Seed, which is the Messiah of every Jew and every believer in the fidelity of Truth and the truthfulness of faith.

DOES GOD WANT BROTHERS TO KILL BROTHERS?

If not God, then who is the perpetrator of the present warfare and lack of understanding? The present fleshly warfare surely comes from Satan the destroyer who uses the ignorance of mankind to trick them into using themselves to murder one another.

WHILE WE WAR IN THE FLESH WE HAVE NO VICTORY IN THE SPIRIT

As it is written,

> "The kingdom of heaven suffereth violence, and the violent take it by force". Matthew 11:12b and; 'The weapons of our warfare are not physical but are mighty through God to the pulling down of strongholds and the casting down of imaginations", Hebrews 12:14–15

and again;

> 'We wrestle not against flesh and blood but against principalities, against powers, against the rulers of the darkness of this age and against spiritual hosts of wickedness in the heavenlies.' Ephesians 6:12

NOTICE THAT THE ENEMY IS A SPIRITUAL ENEMY

A spiritual enemy must be overcome with spiritual weapons instead of physical weapons, which we rather do away with according to the prophecies of old. We beat our swords into agricultural implements:

> "Finally, my brethren, be strong in the Lord, and in the power of his might. Put on the whole armour of God, that ye may be able to stand against the wiles of the devil. For we wrestle not against flesh and blood, but against principalities, against powers, against the

rulers of the darkness of this world, against spiritual wickedness in high places.

Wherefore take unto you the whole armour of God, that ye may be able to withstand in the evil day, and having done all, to stand. Stand therefore, having your loins girt about with truth, and having on the breastplate of righteousness; And your feet shod with the preparation of the gospel of peace; Above all, taking the shield of faith, wherewith ye shall be able to quench all the fiery darts of the wicked. And take the helmet of salvation, and the sword of the Spirit, which is the word of God: Praying always with all prayer and supplication in the Spirit, and watching thereunto with all perseverance and supplication for all saints; Ephesians 6: 10–18

'PRAYING ALWAYS' - CAN WE DELETE THE DARKNESS?

(See page 131)

So it is with our words, which we now use to build one another up in the Truth of the good news (known as the gospel) and in the holiness of Godly co-operation so that we have no reason to weep any more except it be for joy itself. Now we have a choice, to believe or not to believe, to receive or not to receive, that is the question. Will we serve the God of love who created all things and who forgives all those who ask Him to forgive or will we continue to serve the god of hatred who promotes violence and self-destruction?

BUT IS IT EVER 'POLITICALLY CORRECT' TO QUESTION THE IDEOLOGIES OF OTHERS?

Perhaps we should cite the many warning voices that were ignored during the ascendancy of National Socialism, which seemed to be filled with hate and threatening.

Ignoring these voices ended up in the experience of NAZI terrors that plunged almost the whole world into the bloodiest conflict ever experienced until that time.

THE OTHER VOICES

(see page 93)

If Satan was behind that dreadful conflict, perhaps we should ask ourselves just who is behind the other voices that have said 'Hitler was on the right track but just didn't finish the job'?

The above sentiment has been expressed recently by several of the present enemies of Israel.

We might ask ourselves, "Where does Islam in general stand on such issues?"

Would moderate Muslims ever join in Nazi style attempts at world domination?

Fundamental honesty is surely a good thing (see page 46 and for "the dangers of the Fundamentalist name-tag', see pages 124-127)[.]

If indeed we wish to follow the Instructions of God the Creator, how can we blame others who also wish to fully submit? Does Islam not mean 'submission'?

If we have access to truly inspired writings, we would be hypocritical not to follow their teachings.

The key of course is to make sure that we are truly hearing from God and are not being deceived by erroneous writings inspired by some spirit other than God the Creator.

It seems that most fundamentalist practitioners are at least honest in their attempts to obey the literal writings, assuming them to be 'from God'.

Note: Because the god 'Allah' is NOT the same spiritual being as Yahweh ('Jehovah God') written of in the Bible, these two are of necessity in direct opposition. Only ONE of them can be the true AUTHOR OF CREATION and the other must of necessity be the ruler of the darkness, i.e. Satan - the adversary.

THE INSPIRATION OF THESE SPIRITUAL BOOKS

There is no doubt that the Torah, the Tenach, the Naviim the Kethubim, the New Testament and the Koran are each 'inspired' by some spiritual being or beings. The question is, "Which of these books were inspired by God and which were inspired by the adversary?"

WILLFUL PRIDE OR HUMBLE TRUTH?

How long can an honest man willfully allow his own pride to perpetrate and hold satanic deceptions in his mind?

How long before a humble conscience of truth is released and allowed to admit, 'I was deceived, and I have sinned against God!—God forgive me and have mercy on me—a sinner!'

If we ask God, through the Spirit of Truth in Jesus Christ to sever the cords of deception, we know that He is faithful to answer the call of the humble and the sincere.

It is an individual's personal choice, just as He says, 'Choose you this day whom you will serve'.

"Choose life or choose death, for if you be contrary to Me, I will be contrary to you".

Yet again I exhort you, 'Choose life'.

SATAN OPPOSES FUNDAMENTAL HONESTY BUT WHO IS IN OPPOSITION TO ISLAM?

Some religious people may never have the courage to honestly investigate for themselves this question of truth because they are concerned what others might think of them. Some care more for the approval of men rather than the approval of God and where their eternity will be spent–forever.

Long before Mohammed began directing his followers to force the so-called 'truth of Islam' on all others and to loot and kill whenever seemingly desirable or necessary—with dozens of directives to attain that end, there was a new and diametrically opposed teaching spreading like wildfire around the world. Perhaps Islam was created specifically to oppose this message of peace.

This new doctrine was mostly spread by Jewish disciples of a man whose teachings were backed up by God through astounding miracles of healing and many words of peace and love.

WHO WAS THIS MAN?
WHO IS THIS MAN?

The young Jewish teacher called Y'shua or Jesus of Nazareth, the Messiah of Jew and gentile alike, exhorted his followers (and still exhorts his present day followers), thusly.

"Love your enemies, bless them that curse you, do good to them that hate you, and pray for them which despitefully use you and persecute you."

This was a new concept indeed for our warring world and the followers of Y'shua came to understand that they were fighting not against physical enemies but against all the real spiritual beings that constantly caused wars and strife all throughout the world.

THE REAL WAR IS AGAINST
SPIRITUAL BEINGS

The war is against fallen angels that have been putting

deceiving concepts and ideologies into the minds of people everywhere, since the days of Adam, the original man.

"For we wrestle not against flesh and blood, but against (spiritual) principalities and powers, against the rulers of the darkness of this world, against spiritual wickedness in high places"

These principalities are allowed to exist (and to keep their strength) because of sinfulness.

"Because of the transgression of a land many are its princes; but by a man of understanding and of knowledge, the state thereof shall be prolonged." Proverbs 28:2

BUT, God said this: "If My people, which are called by My name, shall humble themselves, and pray, and seek My face, and turn from their wicked ways; then will I hear from heaven, and will forgive their sin, and will heal their land." 2Chronicles 7:14

Nowadays these deceiving spirits are often referred to as 'demons', or in New-age terminology 'daemons', which is an old Greek word with the root meaning of 'voices'. Influences in the mind?

HOW SHOULD WE THEN DIRECT OUR OWN THOUGHTS AND PRAYERS?

2 Corinthians 10: 3–6 teaches us: "Casting down imaginations, and every high thing that exalteth itself against the knowledge of God, and bringing into captivity every thought to the obedience of Christ;" - We must remember that 'people' are not the real enemy. - For though we

walk in the flesh, we do not war after the flesh: All the 'People of the Book' should remember that our battle is not against flesh and blood but against principalities and powers; against spiritual wickedness in high places and not against people who are made in the image of the God. - For the weapons of our warfare are not carnal, but mighty through God to the pulling down of strong holds;

AND ARE WE TO RESIST THE WICKED SPIRITS AND DEAL WITH THEIR DISOBEDIENCE?

"And having in a readiness to revenge all disobedience, when your obedience is fulfilled"

All the angels of creation and all mankind should be worshipping and obeying the God of Abraham, Isaac and Jacob. These fallen angels are in total disobedience to God!

SO WHERE ARE ALL THESE DEMONS NOW?

According to 'The Book', there is one real 'adversary' who is in control of legions of demons.

By that we understand that Satan is an actual and real spiritual being who, with his legions of fallen angels (demons) tries to detrimentally influence the thoughts, imaginations, minds, hearts, loyalties and actions of all mankind to mimic their own rebellion. "Be sober, be vigilant; because your adversary the devil, as a roaring lion, walketh about, seeking whom he may devour: Whom resist stedfast in the faith, knowing that the same afflictions are accomplished in your brethren that are in the world". (1Peter 5:8–9)

RESIST THEM! BUT HOW?

(See page 102*)*

The very first murderer was Cain, the son of Adam. After Cain had murdered his brother, he was told by God that if he did not do well then, 'sin crouches at the door, desiring him' and that he should rule over him. Surely the door was the door of his heart, but on which side of the door was the demonic spirit crouching? Was it like a dog scratching for entrance or a like dog whining to be allowed to manifest its nature from within? Or is the sin nature like lice in the flesh or like flies that buzz around the brain—or all of these?

God firstly spoke to the first man Adam and asked him, "Where are you?"

God spoke to the second man Cain and asked him, "Where is your brother?"

WHERE DO I STAND WITH GOD?

We must first ask ourselves honestly where we stand with God, for it is senseless to try to hide from the all seeing Father of Lights, with whom there is no variance or shadow of turning.

WHERE DOES MY BROTHER
STAND WITH GOD?

If we are right with God, we should next ask ourselves, 'where is my brother?' and how can I help him to be closer to God? Cain lied and asked God, 'am I my brother's keeper?' but Jesus commanded us to Love God and to love our neighbors as ourselves.

HOW DIFFERENT ARE THE IDEALS
OF THE FOLLOWER OF SATAN?

Satan opposes (opposes the command of Y'shua to love one another). Satan is the 'liar' and the 'deceiver' who wants to spread destruction and death throughout mankind. Satan is the murderer and the terrorist who tries to deceive and influence the minds of gullible men and women and tries to twist the thoughts and decisions of mankind from good into evil. His nature is rebellion to God and hatred of any that desire to love and to serve the God of Israel.

Are Satan's 'voices' being used to encourage SBT attacks? Many voices in the secular and Arab/Islamic world have defended the SBT attacks (suicide bomb terrorist attacks) as a justified response to American support for the so-called "Little Satan"—Israel. Sacrifice Israel, this line of thinking goes, and America will no longer be a target of the terrorists. Yet such a course of action would only have the opposite effect.

We know that Satan is a real spiritual being who attempts to use deception, pride, religion, traditions, etc. to influence and control the actions of well-meaning people and murderers alike.

Satan is not a country or regime but he does actually exist as a kind of grand master of the puppet masters who influence minds by 'pulling the strings and pushing the buttons' from behind the scenes, of those who unquestioningly accede to their thought like suggestions.

CHRISTIAN (AND JEWISH) PRAYERS

"If My people, which are called by My name, will humble themselves and pray, and seek My face, and turn from their wicked ways, then will I hear from heaven and will forgive their sins and will heal their land." 2 Chronicles 7:14 (Divrei Ha-Yamim 7:14).

GOD GAVE US A 'FORMULA' FOR HEALING OUR LAND. BELIEVE IT!

Because of the sin of the land, its troubles are increased; but by a man of wisdom and knowledge they will be put out like a fire. Proverbs 28:2 (BBE)

FIRST: CLEANSE YOURSELF AND YOUR PRAYER PARTNERS FROM ALL SIN

In a private place, perhaps while actually washing your physical being, you have already enumerated and have asked daily for forgiveness for specifics in the following.

- Omissions
- Transgressions
- Iniquities
- Blasphemies
- Unclean tongue
- Presumptions and Assumptions
- Then you renounced whatever was brought to mind by the Holy Spirit e.g. Anger, Unforgiveness, Resentment, Bitterness, Hypocrisy, etc.
- Then you asked for the washing and renewing of the Holy Spirit
- Then you asked for the washing of the blood of Jesus
- Then you asked for the purifying cleansing of the fire of the Holy Spirit
- Then as you dried your face perhaps you asked for new programming in purity, holiness, goodness and virtue similar to the inner programming of Enoch who walked with God.
- Then you asked for the healing of the Balm of Gilead and the healing of the Holy Spirit

THANK GOD AND PRAISE GOD FOR ALL THINGS AND FOR REVELATION SPECIFICS.

'Blessed be the Lord who sets His people free from all of the bondages of the wicked'.

Thank God for guidance through His Holy Spirit. Thank and Praise God for answers to past prayers. Thank God that you are hidden in Christ and that the wicked cannot touch you. Acknowledge that God is protecting you and your loved ones from enemy attacks.

PRAY FOR YOURSELF

Pray that the Spirit of Truth will rest upon you and live in you and manifest through you.

Pray also for your prayer partners and for the Body of Christ in like manner.

SATAN IS THE AUTHOR OF ALL FALSE RELIGIONS

The people that Satan deceives seem to be influenced to make themselves as enemies to other people who may, or may not, be personally deceived. Remember that they are only deceived puppets of Satan's purposes. The puppets are not the real enemy because if a puppet is destroyed it can easily be replaced by another puppet.

THE REAL ENEMIES ARE THE
FALLEN ANGELS AND THE
PERSON OF SATAN HIMSELF

The puppet master called Satan is a very real spiritual being who makes himself the adversary of mankind and who directs his fallen angels to use false 'religions' as a means to influence the minds and decisions of men and to cause men to fight with men. Satan cares not for his puppets. This war then, is to win the hearts of men to practice Truth and Love as a way of life instead of manifesting the deceptions of Satan. Recognize then that even Hitler was not the real enemy of the Jews. Hitler was only a puppet utilized by the spirit of anti-Semitism, as directed by 'the adversary', Satan. When Hitler destroyed himself, Satan looked around for other puppets to do his will.

The spirit of anti-Semitism still lives in the hearts of those people who listen to Satan's demonic spirits and heed his ideas and allow their thought patterns to be established as directed by him.

In other words hatred of the 'People of the Book' exists only in the hearts of those who have become the puppets of Satan. Osama bin Laden was likewise only a puppet of the real adversary. Was he also backed by the freedom-hating nations? There is no doubt about it.

Are these freedom-hating nations then the true enemy? Or are they not also just puppets of Satan and his spirit forces? Therefore pray to set the puppets free from Satan's mind-controlling deceptions. Warfare Prayers should be directed at bringing down the spirits of hatred and disbelief that are principalities and powers in the countries where the people are in bondage to cruel masters of false religion and despotism.

"And having in a readiness to revenge all disobedience, when your obedience is fulfilled."

PRAYING FOR EXTRA PROTECTION IS AN ABSOLUTE NECESSITY

*FIRST and afterwards, guard by asking the Lord for SPECIAL PROTECTION from demonic counterattacks directed through family members, friends, acquaintances, business associates, adverse circumstances and the actions of others.

*ASK ALSO FOR THE GIFT OF REPENTANCE,

Ask, because, without the Gift of Repentance, you cannot win! * Ask first for yourself and then for others. "In meekness instructing those that oppose themselves; if God peradventure will give them repentance to the acknowledging of the truth" 2Timothy 2:25

PRAY ALWAYS IN THE NAME OF JESUS CHRIST

Give thanks and acknowledgement, to God the Father with rejoicing for the grace of God that your name is written in the Book of Life. Rejoice in the gift of Salvation and NOT because you have been given authority over the spirits you are about to come against.

> "And the seventy returned again with joy, saying, Lord, even the devils are subject unto us through thy name. And he said unto them, I beheld Satan as lightning fall from heaven. Behold, I give unto you power to tread on serpents and scorpions, and over all the power of the enemy: and nothing shall by any means hurt you. Notwithstanding in this rejoice not, that the spirits are subject unto you; but rather rejoice, because your names are written in heaven.

> Luke 10:17–20

You have authority and you have work ahead of you, but the counterattacks are real!

PRAY AGAINST THE DECEPTIVE SPIRITS RATHER THAN AGAINST THE PEOPLE!

The demons originating from the East are mainly the religious fruits of Babylonian bondage whereas in the West the demons working (for example) through Hollywood script writers, immoral politicians and the cults have been creating havoc in libertine bondage and the self-destructive stubbornness of pseudo-rights organizations, etc.

Perhaps it is a spirit of stubbornness or pride that keeps so many people in bondage to a religion they don't actually fully agree with! These spirits can be prayed against to set your religious friends free! Say directly to the spirits, "THE LORD REBUKE YOU".

Pray constantly along these lines, even as David prayed against his enemies in the psalms.

- Let the spirit of deception in——(named friend) be as the wax that melts in the fire. See it melt, saying to it, "THE LORD REBUKE YOU"
- "Let stubborn pride be gone from me, my friends and all my associates as smoke that blows away and is dispersed in the wind." See it disperse. "Thank You Lord for a humble heart."
- "Let false doctrine be as the grass that withers and dies or as a salted dandelion." See it withering. Let it be deleted forever as unwanted virus spyware is deleted from a computer.
- "Let the roots of (——-) false religion be as rottenness from this day forth." See it waste away.
- "Let the spirits of Lust (which try to drive these young

men to imagine, yearn, long and lust for the falsely promised paradise of 70 'houris' and sexual eternity) be carried into non-existence as ashes scattered in a river." Just as Michael, the archangel admonished the evil one, so admonish these evil spirits directly saying, "THE LORD REBUKE YOU."

- Let demonically inspired sexual imaginations be cast down so that no more sexual energy can be directed into the martyr syndromes of Jihad or to any other demonic scheme or purpose. Admonish them, saying, "THE LORD REBUKE YOU."

- *Pray blessings for others who have similar problems to yourself* being also encouraged that, should the enemy manage to block your words, such blessings will return to benefit you, but if the wicked spirits fail to block the blessing and the blessings land and manifest with those you are praying for, then the Lord will be pleased to reward you in like manner.

"And into whatsoever house ye enter, first say, Peace be to this house. And if the son of peace be there, your peace shall rest upon it: if not, it shall return to you again." Luke 10: 5–6

WICKED THOUGHTS AND IMAGINATIONS

- Let wicked thoughts and imaginations become like the grass that grows on the rooftops of Israel, which grass dries up, withers in the sun and dies. Picture it and see it withering away.

- Likewise deal with the spirits of Antichrist, Hate, Fanaticism, Terrorism and Murder, etc.

- As Jesus cursed the fig tree and it brought forth no more fruit, so speak against the spiritual root of the tree of Islamic Deception and the violence of jihad so that it bears no more fruit.

- "Let the spirits of religious deception be bound as a man bound in chains of steel. Let these unclean spirits be bound with the cords of the love of Jesus and given to Him to dispose of."

- "Let the spirit of error be chased from the doctrines of all people throughout…(Name city or district) who sincerely want to love and serve God the Creator."

- "Let divisiveness strike at the heart of each physical and spiritual organization controlled by Satan or his puppets, knowing the Scripture"…for a house divided against itself must fall"

- Pray specifically for division amongst the demonic organizations and their puppets in the district of… (Name city). Admonish them, saying, "THE LORD REBUKE YOU".

DISENCHANTING THE ENCHANTED

- Let the followers of false religions and demons become 'DISENCHANTED' with them.
- Pray this: "Let all demonic 'chanted words' from devotees of false religions be cancelled," SPECIFICALLY... name your local cults for disbandonment.
- Let the... 'enchantments', incantations, hexes, vexes, spells, oaths and curses begin to dissipate away to ineffectuality like smoke blown away into nothingness by the wind. (See it)
- "In the authority of the Lord Jesus Christ, we cancel this day, the power of all demonically inspired exhortations and incantations in the city of... "
- "Let the words and enchantments of all witches, warlocks, sorcerers, necromancers, antichrist spirits and the like in the city of...be like wooden arrows that are broken into pieces and fall to the ground and are swept down to the lake of fire (see them) but let righteous Christian prayers be like (spiritual) bullets that strike their mark and set the captives free."

"LET THERE BE DIVISION WITHIN THE KINGDOM OF DARKNESS!"

And if a kingdom be divided against itself, that kingdom cannot stand. And if a house be divided against itself, that house cannot stand. And if Satan rise up against himself, and be divided, he cannot stand, but hath an end. Mark 3: 24–26

"Heavenly Father, in the name of Jesus we ask that, just as the Midianites in the days of Gideon, fought one against the other, so let the minions of darkness be divided and fight one against the other! As You delivered the Midianites into the hand of Gideon in days of old, so deliver these wicked principalities into our hand this day O Mighty God! As every man's sword was against his fellow in the days of Gideon, so let every wicked principality fight one with each other in this time, but protect Your servants from any harm O Lord! Thank you Father!"

" ...and the LORD set every man's sword against his fellow, even throughout all the host: and the host fled... And the men of Israel...pursued after the Midianites." Judges 7: 22- 23

NAME AND FORBID

- Name and Forbid each of the named wicked spirits from continuing to influence the minds of their puppets in the district of…(Name of area, organization, town[,] etc.). See the puppet strings being cut! Let the Sword of the Spirit cut these dark spiritual connections.

- "Let divisiveness strike at the heart of each physical and spiritual organization controlled by Satan or his puppets, knowing the Scripture," "for a house divided against itself must fall."

- Name those individuals who are to be set free from false doctrines. Let them see real visions of the Lord Jesus and let them have dreams unto right paths.

- Pray to the Lord of the Harvest and ask for laborers to be sent into the harvest fields of your acquaintances to witness of the Truth to them in ways they will be enabled to receive.

- Ask that favour towards the gospel Truths be put into the hearts of those you pray for.

- Ask the Holy Spirit to draw those you are naming for salvation to Himself, knowing that no-one comes into the knowledge of salvation except those that are drawn by Him.

- Ask the Lord to guide all the actions of your relationship with those you pray for and those you witness to. What will they know by your love?

- Name yourself also for total freedom from error and that the spirit of Truth would manifest in and through you in much love.

- Ask God the Father, in Jesus name, to lead you in the way of righteousness and to keep you from temptation, thanking Him for granting you repentance unto salvation.

- Pray that God draws your friend to Him by His Holy Spirit so that your friend will know the Truth and will be set free!
- Pray that the hinderers be hindered as one who rolls a boulder and it rolls back upon himself.
- "Let those demonic spirits who send counterattacks against us be as those whose own feet are caught in the snares they have set and as those who fall into the pit they have dug, but keep Your servants safe from their devices O Lord our God."
- "O Lord forgive those people who have been honestly deceived. They did not know or even understand what they were doing. Give them a chance to repent and accept Your Truth."
- "Thank you Lord for Your grace and for Your mercy towards those people who were Your enemies and who attacked Your people in error."
- Pray for repentance to be granted to yourself and those whom you are interceding for. Pray for mercy for those who have erred.
- "We pray for mercy for those people who have sent curses against your people O Lord. We know that, as he who rolls a boulder and it rolls back upon his own head, these curses shall return upon their own heads, but let them be accompanied by the knowledge of the Truth, a hunger for the Word of God, a desire for personal salvation, the love of Jesus Christ and a spirit of repentance to enable them to turn and give their lives to You almighty God."
- "Protect us O Father and keep us as the apple of Your eye. Let no weapon formed against us prosper. If the enemy

comes against us one way, let them flee away seven ways, with their feet on slippery ground and chased about by the Angel of the Lord! Hide us under the shadow of Your wing and be merciful to us. Glorify Your Holy name by giving Your servants the victory in the name of Y'shua, the Messiah of the Jews and the Bridegroom of the Bride."

ARE WE TO FIGHT AGAINST THE EVIL ONE?

"…the kingdom of heaven suffereth violence, and the violent take it by force." Matthew 11:12

"Be sober, be vigilant; because your adversary the devil, as a roaring lion, walketh about, seeking whom he may devour: Whom resist stedfast in the faith, knowing that the same afflictions are accomplished in your brethren that are in the world". (1Peter 5:8–9)

Praising the God of Israel can win the battle, for the Lord inhabits the praises of His people.

EXAMPLES OF JEWISH PRAYERS THAT GLORIFY THE GOD OF ISRAEL ALONE

"Magnified and sanctified be the name of God throughout the world which He has created according to His will. May He establish His kingdom during the days of your life and during the life of all of the house of Israel, speedily, yea soon; and say, ye, Amen".

"May His great name be blessed forever and ever".

"Exalted and honored be the name of the Holy One, blessed be He, whose glory transcends, yea is beyond all praises, hymns and blessings that man can render unto Him; and say ye, Amen".

"O Lord/ Guard my tongue from evil and my lips from speaking guile,/ And to those who slander me, let me give no heed./ May my soul be humble and forgiving unto all./ Open Thou my heart, O Lord, unto Thy sacred Law,/ That Thy statutes I may know and all Thy truths pursue./ Bring to naught designs of those who seek to do me ill;/Speedily defeat their aims and thwart their purposes/ For Thine own sake, for Thine own power,/ For Thy holiness and Law,/ That Thy loved ones be delivered,/ Answer us, O Lord, and save with Thy redeeming power."

"May our prayer come before Thee. Hide not Thyself from our supplication, for we are neither so arrogant nor so hardened, as to say before Thee, O Lord our God and God of our fathers, 'we are righteous and have not sinned'; verily, we have sinned".

"We have turned away from Thy commandments and Thy judgments that are good, and it has profited us naught. But Thou art righteous in all that has come upon us for Thou has acted truthfully, but we have wrought unrighteousness".

"What shall we say before Thee, O Thou who dwellest on high and what shall we declare before Thee, Thou who abidest in the heavens? Dost Thou not know all things, both the hidden and the revealed?"

"Thou knowest the mysteries of the universe and the hidden secrets of all living. Thou searchest out the heart of man, and probest all our thoughts and aspiration. Naught escapeth Thee, neither is anything concealed from Thy sight." "May it therefore be Thy will, O Lord, our God and God of our fathers, to forgive us all our sins, to pardon all our iniquities, and to grant us atonement for our transgressions."

PRAY FOR PROTECTION FROM COUNTERATTACK! WITH MUCH THANKSGIVING!

Pray heavily for protection from retaliation by displaced spirits.

- Plead the Blood of Jesus and, in the power and authority of the Name of Jesus Christ of Nazareth who came in the flesh and who was crucified and who rose on the third day.
- Forbid such spirits to attack you, your loved ones, their loved ones or any of the affairs of yourself or of those

named. Rebuke them, saying, "THE LORD REBUKE YOU".

-
- Name each one of those for whom you are requesting protection.
- Pray thusly, "Cover our heads in the day of battle and let the enemy search in vain to locate us, for we are hidden in Christ. Thank you Lord!"
- "Keep us as the apple of your eye, hide us under the shadow of your wings and cause us to walk in the unity of agreement for submission to the present purposes of God."
- GIVE THANKS for the protection of God and the intercession of the saints.
- Pray using scriptural principles, "Let the Angel of the Lord encamp round about us, our loved ones and their loved ones and all of our affairs and those who help us in any way."
- Decree thusly, "As Jezebel was cast down by those she'd made into eunuchs, and was eaten by the dogs, so let the morally corrupt spiritual entities over this area be cast down and destroyed." "Cause us to share your opinion of their abominable behaviour O Lord!"
- "If the enemy comes against us one way they shall be scattered and flee away in seven directions, with their feet on slippery ground while the Angel of the Lord chases them."
- Decree in His authority, "Let these unclean spirits be as those who turn their backs on the archers, having their feet on slippery ground and chased about by the angel of the Lord."
- Ask for protection. "As you protected and prospered Job

in his latter days so protect us with a hedge of protection O merciful Lord. Let no weapon formed against us prosper."

- "As you stood between the Israelites and the Egyptians in the days of the Exodus as a pillar of fire by night and a pillar of smoke by day, so that the Israelites were safe, so protect us from our enemies O Lord, in Jesus' name we pray! Thank You Father!"

- GIVE THANKS for the protection given to those you have specifically prayed for.

- "As You delivered the Israelites from their enemies in those days, so deliver your people in this day O most gracious and merciful Father."

- "As King Ahasuerus was furious with Haman, who was harassing Queen Esther, so let your fury rise up against the adversary that afflicts your people, the Bride of Christ. Lord, deal with the adversary and his fallen angels as King Ahasuerus dealt with Haman."

- "Keep us in the way of righteousness and cause us to manifest the nature of our Lord Jesus Christ in all things and at all times, being in agreement as one with your Spirit of unity." Thank you for granting us repentance dear God.

- GIVE THANKS to God the Father for sending His angels to carry out your requests.

Without ongoing prayer, something along the lines of the preceding, one might expect to be harassed with heavy and bothersome difficulties as there are likely to be attempted 'counterattacks' through circumstances and people which and who are being directed by their spiritual puppet masters to create spiritual and physical problems for the intercessor.

Always remember, "If God is for us, who can be against us?"

EXAMPLES OF ISLAMIC OR MUSLIM PRAYERS

The following excerpts from sermons preaching hate of Jews and "infidels" are taken from the records of the ICEJ NEWS SERVICE, which provides news and comment on Middle East affairs. (http://www.icej.org)

> "Official television stations of four different Arab countries—including Jordan—broadcast sermons last Friday with nearly identical prayers to Allah to bring destruction to Jews, Americans and other infidels."

The live broadcasts on the official TV stations in Jordan, Yemen, Iraq and Saudi Arabia all contained similar calls for the destruction of Jews and their supporters, an indication of how standardized such prayers have become in the Arab/Muslim world.

"O Allah, help your mujahidin servants in Iraq, Palestine, Afghanistan, and elsewhere on the land of Allah. O Allah, give them a clear victory," the Iraqi imam prayed. "O Allah, strengthen them and give them victory over their enemy. O Allah, destroy the Jews and Americans for they are within your power; shoot down their warplanes, drown their ships, weaken their power, and abort their designs."

"O Allah," broadcast the state-run Saudi TV outlet, "strengthen Islam and Muslims. O Allah, protect the religion; destroy the enemies of Islam, the tyrants, and the corrupt; close the Muslims' ranks; and give wisdom to their leaders. O Allah, extend your support to the mujahidin everywhere. O Allah, help them score victory in Palestine, Khashmir, and Chechnya. O Allah, destroy the tyrant Jews and their supporters for they are within your power."

"O Allah, give victory to Islam and Muslims, support those supporting Islam, and humiliate those disappointing Muslims," prayed the imam on Yemeni TV. "O Allah, give victory to the mujahidin everywhere. O Allah, destroy the Jews and their supporters. O Allah, destroy the Christians and their supporters for they are within your power."

The most surprising broadcast, however, came on Jordan's official Channel One TV. "O Allah, strengthen Islam and Muslims and humiliate infidelity and infidels," the Muslim preacher stated. "O Allah, destroy the Jews and the aggressors. O Allah, shake the ground under them and show them a black day. O Allah, give victory to the mujahidin everywhere."

All four broadcasts were monitored and translated by FBIS, a US government translation service, and distributed by IMRA, an Israeli media-monitoring firm.

One might ask, "Why are these prayers, chants (enchantments) and curses so violently oriented towards 'non-believers' and especially towards Jews, Christians, and Americans?"

WHAT IS THE MAIN OR ROOT CAUSE OF ANTI-AMERICAN BIGOTRY AND HATRED?

The main root cause of the alarming level of anti-American hatred in many parts of the world lies in militant Islamic fundamentalist theology, propaganda and its vision of world conquest. Is this because USA seems almost like a world policeman in the way of the zealot's vision of conquest?

WHERE DID THIS DESTRUCTIVE THINKING ORIGINATE?

(See Appendix: B)

Where do mosquitoes originate if not in stagnant waters where larvae gain strength to mature into adult mosquitoes, hungry for blood? Mosquitoes are not interested in negotiations. They just want your blood. Mosquitoes cannot change their nature but prayer can bring spiritual forces to bear that can bind the principalities of demonic ideologies and thereby discourage their murky teachings where terrorist larvae are breeding. Mosquitoes don't breed in clean running streams.

DEATH TO ALL INFIDELS!

Because of the teachings in the Koran, many Islamic sects promote in their mosques the Koranic teachings of violent opposition to ALL other religions, monotheistic or not (See Appendix: B).

> Koran (the Cow) 2:191: And kill them wherever you find them., and drive them out from whence they drove you out, and persecution is severer than slaughter., and do not fight with them at the Sacred Mosque until they fight you in it, but if they do fight you, then slay them; such is the recompense of the unbelievers.

Koran (the Family of Imran) 3:151: We will cast terror into the hearts of those who disbelieve, because they set up with Allah that for which He has sent down no authority, and their abode is in the fire, and evil is the abode of the unjust.

> Koran (the Women) 4:89: They desire that you should disbelieve as they have disbelieved, so that you might be all alike; therefore take not from among them friends until they fly their homes in Allah's way.; but if they turn back, then seize them and kill them wherever you find them, and take not from among them a friend or a helper.

Koran (The Immunity) 9:5: "Then, when the sacred months have passed, slay the idolaters wherever ye find them, and take them captives, and besiege them and lie in wait for them in every ambush. Then if they repent and establish worship and pay the poor-due, then leave their way free. Lo! Allah is Forgiving, Merciful."

> Koran (the Women) 4:91: You will find others who desire that they should be safe from you and secure from their own people; as often as they are sent back to the mischief they get thrown into it headlong.; therefore if they do not withdraw from you, and (do not) offer you peace and restrain their hands, then seize them and kill them wherever you find them; and against these We have given you a clear authority.

JUST WHAT IS THE GOAL
OF ISLAM TODAY?

The goal of Islam today is world dominance resulting in universal submission to their god 'Allah'. Is there a mosque that doesn't preach universally the necessity of universal submission to Allah?

Though there is a zealous sincerity among fundamental Muslim leaders, the directing force for converting people to Islam seems to be elitism and fear.

Islam is a way of life that dictates every aspect of life—when to pray, what to eat, how to dress, etc. Islam is 'submission' to Allah, but do we not know who the spirit behind the name Allah is?

Give an inch and they'll take a mile! Any step or measure at this time in which the US appears to distance itself from its democratic ally Israel will be interpreted by fundamental Muslim extremists as a weakness and an achievement in their terror campaign.

Rendering Israel and Jerusalem more vulnerable would only fuel radical Muslim extremist thinking that their dreams of world conquest are one step closer, and would enhance their ability to draft the masses of ordinary Muslims to their cause.

HOW MANY ISLAMIC ADHERENTS
WERE IN THIS WORLD IN 2006 AD?

According to the CIA Fact Sheet, in 2006 AD there were over 1.6 billion people adhering to Islam and supposedly being influenced by the teachings of the Koran (See Appendix: B).

IT IS A DREAM OF ISLAM
TO DESTROY ISRAEL.

For example, Iranian leader Mahmoud Ahmadinejad is a follower of the ultra-conservative Muslim cleric, Ayatollah Mohammad Taghi Mesbah-Yazdi, who, from his study of the Koran, believes that the Muslim messianic age is about to be inaugurated by the destruction of Israel. President Ahmadinejad has repeatedly said that he feels an aura around him directing his actions.

He believes that chaos will usher in the return of the 12th Imam and that the Shi'ite Messiah, the 12th imam Abul-Qassem Mohammad who "disappeared" in 941, will come back at the end of time as the Mahdi, to herald an era of "Islamic justice".

The seriousness of Ahmadinejad's apocalyptic beliefs are driving his nuclear arms passion, believing that the "Mahdi" can only return if the world is plunged into chaos. It appears that Ahmadinejad is trying his hardest to make the dreams of his Koran-inspired guru come true.

And Iran now has Russian built spy satellites, long distance Shehab III missiles that can reach Israel and Europe with real chemical, and biological or nuclear WMD's. Its population is teeming with tens of thousands of potential suicide bombing martyrs who can fill Hezbollah's ranks.

THE ZIONIST PROPHET ISAIAH IS QUOTED HERE

Look unto Abraham your father, and unto Sarah that bare you: for I called him alone, and blessed him, and increased him. For the Lord shall comfort Zion: He will comfort all her waste places; and He will make her wilderness like Eden, and her desert like the garden of the Lord; joy and gladness shall be found therein, thanksgiving, and the voice of melody.—Isaiah 51:2, KJV

Again:

Thus saith thy Lord the Lord, and thy God that pleadeth the cause of His people, Behold, I have taken out of thy hand the cup of trembling, even of the dregs of the cup of My fury; thou shall no more drink it again: But I will put it in the hand of them that afflict thee; which have said to thy soul. Bow down, that we may go over: and thou hast laid thy body as the ground, and as the street, to them that went over.—Isaiah 51:22 KJV

JEWISH PRAYERS OF
COMPASSION AND MERCY

"O Lord and King who art full of compassion, in whose hand is the soul of every living thing and the breath of all flesh, to Thine all-wise care do we commit the souls of our dear ones, who have departed from this earth. Teach all who mourn to accept the judgment of Thine inscrutable will and cause them to know the sweetness of Thy consolation. Quicken by Thy holy words those bowed in sorrow, that like all the faithful in Israel who have gone before, they too may be faithful to Thy Torah and thus advance the reign of Thy Kingdom upon earth".

"In solemn testimony to that unbroken faith which links the generations one to another, let those who mourn now rise to magnify and sanctify Thy holy name."

"Almighty and eternal Father, in adversity as in joy, Thou, our source of life, art ever with us. As we recall with affection those whom Thou hast summoned unto Thee, we thank Thee for the example of their lives, for our sweet companionship with them, for the cherished memories and the undying inspiration they leave behind. In tribute to our departed who are bound with Thee in the bond of everlasting life, may our lives be consecrated to Thy service. Comfort, we pray Thee, all who mourn. Though they may not comprehend Thy purpose, keep steadfast their trust in Thy wisdom. Do Thou, O God, give them strength in their sorrow, and sustain their faith in Thee as they rise to sanctify Thy name."

Zechariah, son of Bechariah prophesied of the Messiah

saying, "Behold the man whose name is the BRANCH and he shall grow up out of his place, and he shall build the temple of the Lord."

Paul, after calling himself the apostle of the gentiles said:

> "If the root be holy, so are the branches. And if some of the branches be broken off, and you, being a wild olive tree, were grafted in among them, and with them partake of the root and fatness of the olive tree; Boast not against the branches". Romans 11:17–18

THE DANGER OF THE 'RELIGIOUS FUNDAMENTALIST' NAME TAG

The Fundamentalists are being blamed for all these problems and strangely enough, the very term 'Fundamentalists' is becoming an anathema as more and more secular people are beginning to 'realize' (sic) that religious 'fundamentalism' is causing all these political problems and all this bloodshed. More and more the media is laying the blame at the door of 'These Fundamentalists'. Have you noticed that, more and more, all 'fundamentalists' are being lumped together in one despised category? This categorizing assumes that everyone who believes in the fundamental truths contained in any 'Religious Book' is creating all these problems, no matter which Book they are getting their 'fundamental truth' from. How cunning is the evil one to link the two opposing camps by word association so that counterterrorism efforts will be directed at the saints.

The producer of the "What About God?" episode, Bill Jersey, was well known for a 1992 documentary on religious fundamentalism that more or less equated American evangelicals with Muslim terrorists in the Mideast. * One Saudi newspaper, al-Watan, said "Christian fundamentalism is no less dangerous to international peace and security than other forms of religious extremism." That way of thinking will shortly become 'politically correct'.

Notice the surreptitiously increasing use of the word 'FUNDAMENTALISTS' that somehow seems to classify several very different ideologies as the main cause of problems in the world.

*Other NEW-AGE BLOGGERS railed thus * "I just hope this religious fundamentalism, this promotion of ignorance and anti-intellectualism, is the last breath of a dying regressive movement that resist evolution of human culture ." * "A large part of the prejudice is the fault of Moslem fundamentalists...Religious fundamentalism is to be condemned and deleted from human kind whether it is Christian, Jewish or Hindu or Moslem." * "In an earlier post I put forth the idea that... Religious fundamentalism is the greatest threat in the world today. The greatest threat to civilization today is... Religious fundamentalism." * "The religion is immaterial. Christian Muslim, Jewish, Hindu fundamentalism. They're all dangerous." * "Religion and compromise cannot co-exist. It's religion after all. Religion + politics=war." * "Does anyone else notice frightening similarities between the Islamic... fundamentalism's resistance to intellectual advancement abroad and that of Christian fundamentalism here at home? " * "On a final note, Christian fundamentalism is not better than Muslim Extremism."

The simple message is that, with the excuse that terrorists, extremists and fundamentalists are dangerous, Big Brother will be facilitating more and more control, looking over the shoulder of what people are being taught to believe. Fundamentalism will be the new anathema and 'they' will be bringing in anti-terrorist and 'corrective measures' supposedly for our own good.

The sly puppet masters constantly move the media to surreptitiously lay the blame for all the problems and all the troubles in the world, squarely on the shoulders of these 'Islamic fundamentalists, Jewish fundamentalists, the Israelis and their Christian fundamentalist supporters. Pseudo-Christians are also being utilised to demonstrate the evils of fundamentalism.

NOT VERY LONG FROM NOW

When The Lord said that "Wars and rumors of wars shall increase and 'they' shall deliver you up"… etc., just who was He referring to?

Not very long from now, together with amazing modern surveillance techniques, authorities will naturally decide they have to try to address the 'breeding pools of fundamentalism' to stop the fundamentalist leaders from teaching and influencing their listeners in such negative ideologies.

Who will be deciding what is right and allowable?—
The mysterious 'They'?

If ideologies do not coincide with the rules of the ruling elite, these ideologies will be hindered and curtailed. The rationale will be that 'Fundamentalism is an evil that must be eradicated.'

> "And ye shall be hated of all men for my name's sake…
> And when these things begin to come to pass, then
> look up, and lift up your heads; for your redemption
> draweth nigh… Watch ye therefore, and pray always,
> that ye may be accounted worthy to escape all these
> things that shall come to pass, and to stand before the
> Son of man." Luke 21:17 - 36

Pray ALWAYS that you might be accounted worthy to escape all these things.

"Obedience is better than sacrifice." Do you ever obey that command or have you arrogantly assumed that you will automatically be included in the rapture when it happens? *Pray now.

SUMMING UP THE FACTS

To sum up the facts, it was Isaac, the son of Abraham and the father of Israel to be, who was required by God to be offered as a sacrifice. Through Israel came the Messiah who is the greatest blessing the world will ever know. The Messiah was sacrificed as a substitute for you and I, et al.

In short, the blessing was promised to mankind through the seed of Abraham and the seed of Israel. That Seed is the Messiah of every spiritual Jew who receives Him.

BOTH OF THE NATIONS MAY THEREFORE CHOOSE TO PARTAKE

Both of the nations from the sons of Abraham may therefore choose to partake of the promised blessing, which is given freely to everyone who will believe and receive.

ALL NATIONS OF THE WORLD MAY CHOOSE TO PARTAKE AND TO BE GRAFTED INTO THE ROOT.

All the people from all the nations of the world may choose to partake in the blessing, just as promised to Abraham by God!… Praise God!

INTERCESSION AND SPIRITUAL
JUDGEMENT PRAYER ADDENDUM

Have you been plagued by demonic interference in your affairs?

"Know ye not that ye shall judge angels?" 1 Corinthians 6::3

"Casting down...every high thing that exalteth itself against the knowledge of God"

"LORD, You are my rock, and my fortress, and my deliverer; my God, my strength, in whom I will trust; my buckler, and the horn of my salvation, and my high tower. Send out Your arrows, and scatter these wicked spirits. Shoot out Your lightnings, and discomfit them."

Why did Jesus submit to baptism but as a perfect EXAMPLE for new believers to follow?

"Yet Michael the archangel, when contending with the devil he disputed about the body of Moses, durst not bring against him a railing accusation, but said, 'The Lord rebuke thee.'" Jude 1: 9

Why did the Lord say the following, if it were not as an EXAMPLE for us to follow?

And the LORD said unto Satan,' The LORD rebuke thee, O Satan; even the LORD that hath chosen Jerusalem rebuke thee: is not this a brand plucked out of the fire'? Zechariah 3:2

However, fallen angels can only be judged through delegated authority from the Lord Jesus Christ, for ALL authority has been delegated to Him

"All authority has been given to Me in heaven and on earth" Matthew 28:18).

So now this is our reality, "You are of God, little children, and have overcome them; because greater is He who is in you than he who is in the world."1John4:4

"Casting down...every high thing that exalteth itself against the knowledge of God"

IS THERE TROUBLE? SEND THEM DOUBLE! "Let them be confounded that persecute me, but let not me be confounded: let them be dismayed, but let not me be dismayed: bring upon them the day of evil, and destroy them with double destruction." Jeremiah 17:18

Firstly, are you walking in the safety of the Righteousness of Christ? "And having a readiness to revenge all disobedience, when your obedience is fulfilled".

2 Corinthians 10: 6

ASK FOR PROTECTION

BEFORE and AFTER engaging in spiritual warfare, ALWAYS ask the Lord for extra protection from the retaliation of the powers of darkness (see page 112). Pray also for direction from the Lord and, IF you feel you are getting the 'go-ahead' from Him; Command something along these lines: "All spirits of darkness that have, or have had, any involvement with the hindering of my affairs and/or possessions and/or any of the affairs and/or possessions of my relatives, loved ones, colleagues or associates, I address you in the name of the Lord Jesus Christ of Nazareth. Dark spirits, The LORD REBUKE YOU! You spirits that have been involved in any way in stealing from us and those we have named, The LORD REBUKE YOU! Restore our goods according to the principles of Exodus 22."

CANCELLING THE MISSIONS OF THE DARK SPIRITS.

Consider the difference between delegated authority and spiritual power.

A policeman has all the authority of the government behind him but he may need physical backup in order to exercise that authority. We need to ask God for that backup. Also remember, "One can chase a thousand but two can put ten thousand to flight" (Deuteronomy 32:30), and it helps greatly to have someone else of a like mind agree with you. "Where two or three are gathered together in My Name, there am I in the midst of them."—Matthew 18:20. And, "If any two of you shall agree on Earth as touching anything that they shall ask, it shall be done for them."-Matthew 18:19. There is great power in UNITED prayer!

*Ask God to send angels to enforce your decrees:

"Thinkest thou that I cannot now pray to my Father, and he shall presently give me more than twelve legions of angels?" Mat 26:53

Every intercessor should pray as the Lord leads and, if He approves in your case, o gentle reader, this kind of format may be useful to use as an example to delete the darkness:

"You spirits of darkness, we address you in the Name of the Lord Jesus Christ of Nazareth, who rose from the grave on the third day and we command that you immediately cease all your missions against all of us and we command that you go immediately to the Lake of Fire, together with your up-line, all your downline, all your backups, all your replacements, all your associate demons all your tools, time bombs, machinations and devices. The LORD REBUKE YOU! Go immediately without completing your evil assignments and never return. We give these commands in the name of Y'shua ha Mashiach and, by the power of the Blood, the Cross and the Resurrection we command every dark spirit to obey immediately and to never return."

"All dark spirits that are involved in any way in influencing the speaking of evil words, charms, curses, hexes, vexes, spells or the chanting of antichrist enchantments or satanic pulses, vibrations, or mantras; whether by practitioners of Witchcraft or New Age cultists, etc., in the district of (...   ...) are hereby commanded to take your words and all your associated demons with you and go directly and immediately to the Lake of Fire. We say to you dark spirits, "The Lord rebuke you! We hereby cancel all your curses and all your enchantments, etc. We cancel them by the Power of the Blood, the Cross and the Resurrection of the Lord Jesus Christ of Nazareth, who rose from the dead on the third day and in His name all your evil works are cancelled."

"Heavenly Father, we thank you for hearing our words and for supporting our petitions. Glorify Your Holy Name by causing us to triumph over your enemies. Worthy is Your Name Almighty God! Father, send out your lightning against those spirits that have harassed your children. Let our words be as arrows that strike their mark but let all enemy words and enchantments be as broken wooden arrows that fall to the ground and are swept down to the Lake of Fire, together with all the demons and spirits that enabled them. Thank You Father for Your merciful protection and Your everlasting Love! Thank You Lord! Blessed be Your name! AMEN."

APPENDIX

Appendix A:

The Koran (The Cow) 1.[2.189] They ask you concerning the new moon. Say: They are times appointed for (the benefit of) men, and (for) the pilgrimage;

The Islamic calendar is based on LUNAR CYCLES alone, from the time the CRESCENT MOON can be seen from any given area. This Muslim LUNAR calendar was formed in 638 AD and dated from July 16th, 622 AD when Muhammad had migrated from Makkah to Medina to start the original Muslim city-state. This was the origin of the Hijri year of twelve purely LUNAR months.

The Hijri year falls short of the normal calendar year by 11 days, making each of the spring/ summer/ fall/ winter seasons arrive 11 days earlier than the year before. The 'AH' calendar (Anno Hegira) unsuccessfully attempted to replace the 'AD' calendar for world usage.

The most recent attempt to usurp Anno Domini (in the year of our Lord) is to replace 'BC' (before Christ) with 'BCE' (Before Common Era). This proposed change in nomenclature would have allowed 'AD' to be replaced by 'CE' (Common Era) and such attempts still continue to this day.

Anyhow, each Hijri month in the Muslim calendar starts with a sighting of the NEW MOON.

"Efforts for obtaining an astronomical criterion... go back the Babylonian Era, with significant improvements done later by Muslim scientists. - No Hijri software can be 100% reliable and an actual CRESCENT MOON sighting remains essential for fixing important dates such as Ramadhaan." - from 'A modern guide to astronomical calculation of Islamic calendar Times & Qibla' - Berita Publishing 1984 (ISBN: 967–969–009).

Appendix: B:

Historic facts concerning Mohammed and Islam.
http://www.templemount.org/missler.html

Appendix: C:

Allah and YHWH are two very different spirits.
This fact needs to be emphasized to Muslims, Christians and Jews alike.
http://www.menorah.org/allahtrc.html

Headings for easy reference: